23% More Spiritual!

"Miller takes no prisoners as he cuts to the heart of the American obsession with fads, an obsession that is just as strong among Christians as it is among the secular population. Rather than merely list and critique the fads of the last half-century, Miller carefully diagnoses the causes of our obsession and offers solutions for restoring sanity and depth to the American church."

—LOUIS MARKOS
Professor of English, Houston Baptist University,
and author of *Atheism on Trial*

"Miller sheds light on one of the most problematic aspects of American Christianity—its intertwining with the culture of consumerism. After analyzing dozens of overt and subtle instances of acquiescence to the trends of the larger culture, Miller delves into a practical discussion of how Christians can assess their motives and choices in light of their faith. A useful read for clergy and laypeople alike."

—TYRUS CLUTTER
Artist and Associate Professor of Art,
College of Central Florida

"Rod cuts to the chase in this book and critiques the cult of fads because it has had an insidious influence upon the church for a good while and the church needs to be very cautious about false teaching. The core of the problem is that fads are superficial and make empty promises they cannot begin to deliver; fads are often driven by financial motives, and in the end they de facto encourage a life of carnality (stroking one's ego). Rod substantially critiques all of these errors. This topic has sobering implications for serious discipleship in following Jesus and is a much-needed word for today."

—JAMES PARKER III
Director of the Trinity Institute, Tehuacana, Texas

"This book is thought-provoking, wise, and well worth your time. Rod Miller shakes us up by urging us to look closely at our cultural assumptions that new or different is always better . . . Even though Jesus's yoke is easy, and his burden is light, a life of obedience to God and spiritual growth is not instant and takes perseverance."

—**MARY MCCLEARY**
Artist and Regent's Professor Emeritus,
Stephen F. Austin State University

"*23% More Spiritual!* is a deceptively thoughtful book inhabiting a space which is transparently vacuous. Rod Miller helps map our fragmenting cultural and church life and shows us a way forward, which, paradoxically, is the way back. Back to something deeper, something more just, more true, more beautiful, and ultimately more Christian."

—**COLIN M. C. REDEMER**
Vice President of The Davenant Institute
and Professor at Saint Mary's College of California

23% More Spiritual!

Christians and the Fad

Rod Miller

Foreword by Arthur Pontynen

WIPF & STOCK · Eugene, Oregon

Wipf & Stock
An Imprint of Wipf and Stock Publishers
199 W. 8th Ave., Suite 3
Eugene, OR 97401

www.wipfandstock.com

PAPERBACK ISBN: 978-1-7252-8276-6
HARDCOVER ISBN: 978-1-7252-8275-9
EBOOK ISBN: 978-1-7252-8277-3

Manufactured in the U.S.A.   09/30/20

To all my teachers.
No, really, I was listening.
Mostly.

What we want, if men become Christians at all, is to keep them in the state of mind I call "Christianity And." You know—Christianity and the Crisis, Christianity and the New Psychology, Christianity and the New Order, Christianity and Faith Healing, Christianity and Psychical Research, Christianity and Vegetarianism, Christianity and Spelling Reform. If they must be Christians, let them at least be Christians with a difference. Substitute for the faith itself some Fashion with a Christian colouring. Work on their horror of the Same Old Thing.

The horror of the Same Old Thing is one of the most valuable passions we have produced in the human heart—an endless source of heresies in religion, folly in counsel, infidelity in marriage, and inconsistency in friendship. The humans live in time, and experience reality successively. To experience much of it, therefore, they must experience many different things; in other words, they must experience change. And since they need change, the Enemy (being a hedonist at heart) has made change pleasurable to them, just as He has made eating pleasurable . . . We pick out this natural pleasantness of change and twist it into a demand for absolute novelty.

—C.S. LEWIS, *THE SCREWTAPE LETTERS*

The priest was enchanted by her change of heart, though he was of the opinion that her faith might by its very fervor come to border on heresy and even on extravagance. But not being versed in these matters once they went beyond a certain point, he wrote to Monsieur Boulard, the bishop's bookseller, and asked him to send him "something particularly good for a lady who had a very fine mind." As casually as though he were shipping trinkets to savages, the bookseller made up a heterogeneous package of everything just then current in the religious book trade—little question-and-answer manuals, pamphlets couched in the contemptuous language made popular by Monsieur de Maistre, so-called romantic-minded seminarists or reformed blue-stockings. There were titles such as *Think it Over Carefully; The Man of the World at the Feet of Mary; The Errors of Voltaire*; etc.

—GUSTAVE FLAUBERT, *MADAME BOVARY*

Contents

Foreword

IN THIS BOOK, PROFESSOR Miller provides the reader with an uncomfortable but valuable opportunity. He presents ample evidence of a superficial trendiness in contemporary Christian thought and practice, and by doing so provides an opportunity for critical self-reflection.

The need for such critical self-reflection is never easy to accept or pleasant to do. Just as a prophet is never welcome in his own country, a call for critical self-reflection easily provokes resistance. But lacking that openness to self-criticism, the integrity of living a Christian life is imperiled. A lack of self-criticism concludes in a rigid self-parody.

Miller sounds the alarm that despite good intentions, contemporary Christian thought and practice have significantly and tragically conformed to a world that has difficulty in distinguishing between the trivial and the profound, entertainment and reverence. As his Introduction notes, when faith becomes novelty, it is deprived of its Sacred content.

It is easy to condemn that superficiality so characteristic of entertainment and popular culture. It is perhaps more disturbing to note the debasement of college curricula via the establishment of various dogmas and multiple pseudo-intellectual disciplines (often recognizable by the suffix *–studies*). Such foolishness by academics might be shrugged off as the product of an unrealistic, quirky, or radicalized professoriate.

It is much harder to consider that religion, as the source of meaning and value in life, is today similarly afflicted. Nonetheless, with ample evidence, Miller establishes this to be the case. This is not an act of condescending arrogance; it is a humble yet resolute plea to return to seriousness. It is solidly reformational in spirit.

Presented via an accessible narrative, he addresses the problem of confusing a trendy superficiality for genuine spiritual development. The presence of the fad indicates an absence of wisdom, of depth, of profundity. A faddish religion is trivial and destructive.

Miller presents this view by way of three distinct methods: a creative example, a historical record, and an analysis of how this understanding developed. First, he provides the reader with an exemplar of what he is talking about. This is followed by historical examples of how widespread the occurrence of similar narratives has been. He concludes with a deeper analysis of the reasons why they have been accepted, and how we can recover from them.

Both secular and religious institutions reflect sets of ideas about how we should live. A certain stability is to be expected of such institutions, since they are so foundational. At the same time, those institutions are subject to the influences of the moment. As such, their status makes them proponents of a *status quo*, grounded in a dialogue between the past and present. That current *status quo* may be for better or worse.

A problem is that institutions are particularly resistant to self-criticism and self-reflection. As such, the institutions now associated with a superficial trendiness will respond unfavorably to Miller's critique. To be told that they have drifted away from their foundational origins is at odds with their current claim of being foundational.

Although an academic, Professor Miller has elsewhere challenged the foolish trendiness of the contemporary academy. In this book, he tackles the deeper issue of how that academy, and the zeitgeist, has afflicted the substantive importance of faith and Christianity. Neither task is welcomed by those he challenges. Institutions do not reward their critics.

Foreword

So it is as an act of intellectual integrity, and Christian conviction, that such a book is written. Both are long recognized as intrinsic to living a Christian life. In Appendix II, Miller's intentions are explained in reference to the List of Resolutions from Jonathan Edwards. They are neither faddish nor arrogant, nor is this splendid book.

Arthur Pontynen
May 2020

Acknowledgements

THE AUTHOR IS INDEBTED to Ronald K. Miller for insightful comments throughout this project. *Sine patribus, filii pereunt.*

Introduction

THERE ARE MORE EXAMPLES than we might care to recall. How many times have we sat in congregations and wondered just who came up with the idea of having interpretive dance as an element of Sunday worship? Do we like staring at the tatty T-shirts of our music ministers as they perform in flip-flops from atop a platform splashed with lights and constantly increasing decibels? Is the new diet going to be guided by angelic hands? Where did that new, or "new," approach to whatever spiritual issue come from? Do we ever look at the changes and consider what has been gained but also what has been lost? For one example drawn from worship practices: How did we get from sitting seriously in church, dressed seriously—reverently, perhaps—while being led by someone who was not playing, but was leading us, to what has become in many places a sort of happy-clappy concert for Jesus? Why did we think this was a good change? To the point: Do we even think about these changes?

This project found inspiration during a particularly vapid keynote at a conference on faith and the arts. The speaker spent her time speaking about a method of prayer, Praying the Hours—a practice drawn from some medieval Christian traditions. Of course, she had penned the perfunctory book on the subject and with great passion, she explained how good it was to know that when she was praying out the hours in one time zone, other believers were praying in the next hour in the next time zone. The unspoken assumption in her presentation is that this method, this technique, is an improvement. I expected her to say what perhaps might have been more honest: "While we know that some Christians think they are praying the best way, the way that I am suggesting is actually better, more improved, faster, and with 23-percent more efficiency." I'm glad she did not express such hubris, and yet what followed at the end of her presentation took my breath away. During the Q&A, she shared that her career had been in Christian publishing, and then proceeded to outline the past twenty years of what she'd witnessed. She did so with rather a wink and a nod. Christian publishing, she asserted, had all grown from a single root: The Twelve-Step Program. Whereas in the past, people sought guidance from their priest, now we could read a book. Self-help publishing sprang from that, and Christian publishing from it. And that had led, she said wryly, to Old Testament Saints, Irish Saints, and Angels, to name but a few of the recent trends. She even made the damming comment, "The year Irish Saints were big stuff, I could have published my shopping list if it had been printed in green ink!" The implication is that Christian publishing publishes a bunch of superficial tripe that gets sold to superficial consumers. What was astonishing is that she seemed to have not the slightest conception that the book that she had just published, and discussed, was yet another superficial trend.

This is a significant problem for a number of reasons. When we consider the production of some new Christian cultural product, what exactly is being considered, and by whom? Is it always based on the humble and passionate pursuit of truth, of wisdom? Do writers seek divine leading before setting down to write? Producers of Christian products often expect their works to sell. Does the business end of cultural production have an effect upon what is being produced? Furthermore, what is being considered by the consumers of those products? Is there any reflection whatsoever? Much like the culture at large, we Christians also tend to consume rather blindly, making many assumptions, or riding on unspoken assumptions (e.g., newer equals better) and avoiding much reflection. Perhaps the reader might consider how their own purchases are made, what books they decides to read and, perhaps most significantly, what they hope to gain from the reading of those books (or the listening to of those songs, watching of those DVDs, or less commonly, the viewing of those plays or works of art). What *ought* to motivate the Christian when considering engagement with cultural products?

This book looks at the history, problems, and origins of trends; that is, trendiness, or the reckless pursuit of the new, in Christian cultural products. The roots for this mess stem from some very not-Christian thinking that developed in the eighteenth century, were watered in the nineteenth, and flowered during the early twentieth into the noisome blossom that is still with us. Critically, this matters. These desires for the new, the fresh, or the original have spilled over from the world and into the church; they affect much of what we do and how we view culture itself. This trendy desire comes, like all perspectives, from ideas, and ideas have consequences. What we teach, preach, or write in the abstract can manifest itself in ways we may not realize and in ways that ultimately undermine our beliefs, our testimonies, and our lives.

1

The Inferences of Panegyrics

Hey, hey, the light. Look at the light!
It's like, bright, man.

—RAMON

I ONCE HEARD RAMON, a homeless Lebanese man in Pioneer Square, say that God is like a traffic light, sometimes green and sometimes red. And sometimes, yellow. That really struck me because it means that sometimes we can cross the street with God, other times, we have to stop. But then there are occasions when we have to rush, to race, to cross the street in time.

Back in 1988, I remember walking through my campus quad, measuring movement by the slow repetition of my steps. Step. Thought. Step. Thought. The day burned deliberately, it seemed, with a Texan end-of-summer heat. Step. Thought. Step. Pulling me from my musings, an unseasonal, gentle, steamy rain fell about me, mocking my rhythmic steps. Did rain fall more meaningfully back then? Maybe. That day, that gloriously strange day, the rain rolled out of the sky and slid across the paths and greens of my college like mercury on hot steel.

Sure, many attended a college or university in the 80s. Who could claim uniqueness in that? But my experience enveloped a realm of mystery that all but even the most authentic would have received with skepticism. The events of that late September afternoon, a day normal in its start but extraordinary in its end, shaped my heart and my mind. It moved me towards an inner, passionate recognition and authenticity, one that still lingers.

I strolled, pondering that day as earlier it was revealed to me that all my hopes of passing calculus were for naught. That revelation took the form of my professor. He said words, words, and phrases. What did they mean? Homework and test scores. I did not invest myself into the subtext. It was, then, not possible. The words were real, but what could I do? I knew a turning point lay just beyond my feeble perception. Seeking solace, I moved my feet, feeling first the turf, then the pavers, then the tarmac, deep down with each step. My direction lay towards the west. There lay Mandalay, a propitious name for an apartment complex, my own residence, a private sphere, my collegiate womb.

Opening the door, then shutting it quickly, I entered a nexus of quietus. Christ was near, I knew. We always know, don't we? Even when we do not know, we know. Crudely fashioning a lunch for myself, I moved in an automatic way. Anxiously, tension built. Was it the calculus grade? Probably. Maybe. I didn't know then. I absently tossed bread on a plate, a heart-shaped plate; even the mustard seemed to ooze carefully across the yeast-infused sustenance. But other events, distractions, were brought to me, were shown to me.

Kathy. Any sentient human knows that an ended relationship didn't mean the end of all of life. During youth, however, it certainly feels like the world is breaking up. Breaking up. The words stuck in my mind and in my throat. Breaking up. It is what we say, isn't it? And it makes sense as something that had been running, operating smoothly, functioning, gets ruined. Disabled. Broken up. But it isn't up, it is down. My heart told me what it is that we really ought to say: that relationship, that life, had broken *down*. And deep down I knew it, it resonated with a glorious clarity. I could hold onto that clarity. Man, could I hold it.

But.

What.

Now?

Entering the apartment it felt like pushing back a veil; what had been was now broken. My roommate had moved out the previous week. Our cat had died in a tragic accident. Now my life was broken down. Where was Garrett, my roommate? Where was Kathy, my girlfriend? Where was God? I fell to the floor and wept; wept as I had not since being a child. And perhaps I again was a child, a child of God.

But God does not let us rest like that. Someone knocked on the door. After all my other closed doors, this one opened eagerly. Standing there, afternoon light dancing on her grey hair, an elderly black woman reached out to me. It was not so much her words that affected me but my own innate reactions. As she went on, with more and more words, about second chances and magazines and such, I recoiled at my own tenderness. I gave, she received, but really, I did the receiving.

Deeping, the rain folded down, splashing, laughing onto the sidewalk outside my apartment. Could I have known the display and hope that would be demonstrated to me? Throwing myself onto an old sofa, one with a family history, passed down from grandmother, my parents, now to me, I fell into a fitful nap. Dancing in my mind's eye were swirls of circularity, round and round. These were punctuated by booming echoes of thunder, flashes of lightening. It felt to me like the earth roiled beneath me

My inner turmoil took the greater prize. I ran. Feet, unshod, barely able to carry me. But I ran. Up the hill near my apartment, across the parking lot. I ran. Blinded, by rain, storm, wind. Natural. And then, as pelting drops of reality drenched me, washed me, baptized me, I found myself outside an old church. Stone, darkened from rain, thick oaken doors, arches pointing upwards. I entered between thunderclaps. Inside, dark. I heard trumpets, or what sounded like trumpets to me, in that place, at that time. Then emotions, feelings, stone, glass, all crashing around me— and I slept.

I awoke only to find ceiling beams at disjointed angles, odd flashes of light through remnants of stained glass windows, and doors, the carved entry points, blasted aside, open to view. Who can guess why? But now this church had to deal with it. Skeptics might blame the tornado that blew through the town, but still! Such a night of revealed mystery that opened up the endless possibilities, presenting through God's hand in the drama of existence and the beauty of nature's drama. As the morning blast of sunrise refracted through the shards, my soul leapt, each fragment of what I had thought of as myself singing a chorus of granulated perfection with an utterly jejune neo-concept towards a psyche grounded upon an edifice of narrative refinement.

iT wAs as iF
alL
ruleS
weRe
gOnE.

2

Festival of Fads!

Hell is paved with good intentions.

—JOHN RAY, 1670

WE SUSPECT THERE ARE readers who will have read the nonsense in the previous chapter and attempted to draw some spiritual lesson out of it. There isn't one. Or, to be more precise, there is one, but it has nothing to do with the stupidity of those pages. The lesson is: just because we read flowery, mysterious, or hipster prose, we need not think anything valuable is being related. This ought to be an easy lesson for Christians. It isn't.

Of course, that trivial story is a parody and critique of Donald Miller's book, *Blue Like Jazz*. Why did Miller's book make such a big splash, sell so many copies? Because Miller's years of experience, education, ministry, and suffering led to profound understanding, wisdom, and insight of the Bible, Christ, Christians, Discipline, God? Probably not. Did it sell because it was different? Hip? Because it confirms for younger Christians a way to embrace both an ego-stroking postmodernism that legitimizes their own relativistic choices and a form of squishy Christianity while also giving a green light to smoke pot and diss their own churches?[1]

It has been more than a decade since Miller published his book. So how ought we to think about *Blue Like Jazz*? Destined to become a Christian classic? Will this sit on shelves a hundred years from now alongside Augustine's *Confessions*, Luther's *On the Bondage of the Will*, or Lewis's *Mere Christianity*?

To be clear, Miller's book is just one example in a vast store of books and products. Ostensibly, we assume this mountain of publishing and production marks an attempt to make Christianity and the Christian life more intelligible. That is to say, there is an assumption that books written about various aspects of Christianity and the Christian life are done in the hopes of promulgating the truth, the wisdom, that comes from God. Certainly, there is nothing wrong with aspiring to do that. It is a mark in most traditions of Christianity to seek out wisdom from other Christians, to understand how they travailed in the Christian life, and to grow in understanding and wisdom. But is this all that is happening with Miller's book, and many other Christian books?

Or is it a relentless push for the new? Sometimes a book will propose a new sort of thinking, one that proposes a new method for doing things Christians ought to be doing and doing it better. Of course, we Christians are directed to desire to understand more, to grow, to get deeper in all aspects of our faith. But, sometimes, new books attempt something "quicker, faster, more seductive."[2] That is

---

1. It does not seem to us that we are picking on Miller unduly. See the conclusion of chapter 17 of Miller's work: "At the end of the day, when I am lying in bed and know the chances of any of our theology being exactly right are a million to one, I need to know that God has things figured out, that if my math is wrong we are still going to be okay. And wonder is that feeling we get when we let go of our silly answers, our mapped out rules that we want God to follow. I don't think there is any better worship than wonder." I wonder how he got this published. Tragically, there are some Christians who believe this passes for good thinking. Is it possible that Miller may have ever once reflected that his claim, whether "there is any better worship than wonder," might be but another silly answer? We might wish to consider if there are any rules, even "mapped out" ones, that are not *our* rules but are God's. Miller, *Blue Like Jazz*.

2. Yoda, *Empire Strikes Back*, 1980.

not always a good thing. Also, unfortunately, are Americans. Being such simply means that we live in this particular culture and that we are affected by it. We end up, as American Christians, in an oddly troubling place: caught between understanding that the Christian life is about growth, development, and relationship, that it involves self-denial, sacrifice, endurance of suffering, that it changes and adapts as we aspire to become better, wiser, more Christ-like, *and* the American life wherein we seek the next, the better, the bestest of all, that will fix all problems and cure all ills more quickly and with 23-percent more efficiency. This is ironic and deeply troubling. It is ironic as we are at once seeking the eternal, the transcendent, and the permanent, but we swim about in the world which we know cannot satisfy; it is troubling in that we spend an extraordinary amount of time, intelligence (sometimes), and money (frequently) seeking the new better and thing and, as we might expect (or ought to expect), it rarely provides the promised fix. There is something terrifyingly stupid about us as humans that makes us laugh when we see it in others: we know the quick fix is rarely a fix, that advertising and greed often serve to separate us from our money, and yet the appeal is perennial. Notably, this appeal is to all humans, those who follow Christ and those who follow anything else. Perhaps a good thing to remember is that the devil once took the form of a snake and snake oil salesmen are everywhere.

We keep looking, hoping, and putting effort into finding the new better thing when deep down we all know the real path is one of sacrifice, compassion, and, often, suffering. It is perhaps not amiss to refer to this "new better thing" as a trend, a fad. Fads turn out not to be really that new, nor really any better. Usually, they disappear after a splash. But when the disappearance does not happen quickly enough, or the splash is of a notable magnitude, particular fads may leave behind significant damage. Perhaps more to the point for the Christian life: the fad can distract us, can push us off the Way, or slow us down. Sometimes they may push believers from the Way entirely.[3]

---

3. It is not entirely amiss to think of many cults as fads. They promise something that the traditional faith either does not offer or offers with substantial

Before discussing specifically how the fad can corrupt and destroy (chapter 3), it is appropriate to support a critique of the fad with some examples. For, of course, we may well consider constantly updated and changing fads as something related to growth, avoiding stagnation, towards a revival of truth, goodness, and beauty. To build the case against the fad, what follows are a selection of examples from roughly the past hundred years. Many of them, notably, are cringe-inducing. What follows is not an exhaustive lexicon of fads that have befuddled Christians. However, it's quite likely you, dear reader, have indulged in at least one of them. Notable for the fads below is that while they differ in duration and degree of harm, not all of them can be traced to a single teacher or writer. But like any fad, they seem to offer something valuable which then, sometimes, dissipates. Perhaps some will also induce shame and repentance.

Social-Gospel Fad!

There are many places we could start in looking at the fads that were thought so important and meaningful but are now long gone, if not forgotten.[4] The Social Gospel Movement strikes us as a profoundly important example because of its scale, its lack of

---

commitment. And what might be the motives for some to enter cults? The offer (rather, a hope?) of "secret" information, of "more" understanding, of exclusivity? That is to say, they are an appeal to that most base of human corruptions, pride. But of course, it need not be something as dramatic as joining a cult to get believers off of the the Way. Indeed, we are persuaded the more potent threats are those fads that pose as some amazing new way, that make promises, seem easier, and are regarded as harmless.

4. We asked others when they thought Christian fads began. Several suggested starting far back in history. One suggested that Sunday School started as something rather like a fad, another thought we ought to take on the Renaissance, and another suggested that Constantine's myriad changes to Christianity might also be seen as fads. In an effort to keep the argument sharp and closer to home, it seemed efficacious to explore more recent fads. Ultimately, this project aspires to move beyond the question, "How have we screwed up in the past?" to, "How might we tell the difference between fad and a substantial and genuinely profound improvement?"

intellectual and theological rigor, and large effect (both sacred and secular), parts of which might rightly be called disastrous.

The movement started sometime in the mid-nineteenth century. It was an attempt to organize Christians into social activism and may have had roots going back to the Great Awakening. As the Industrial Revolution grew, so too did typically awful working conditions and lots of sufferings that sound familiar still: illiteracy, illegitimacy, health care issues, substance abuse, pollution, economic hardships, and massive urbanization. Some Christians began to feel that something was missing in their practice of Christianity, that portions of what they taught were off the mark, and that they needed to make a deliberate effort to make America a more just culture. This conviction mingled with a good dose of millennialist thinking. With roots as far back as the eighteenth-century pastor and thinker Jonathan Edwards, the millennialist idea was that if a perfect Christian culture could be established, Christ would return.

The Social Gospelers, as they were sometimes called, made some positive contributions. Many of them helped to plant churches in poor, often rural areas, and many fought for abolition and then again for the rights of the recently freed slaves. There were concerns with rising poverty, economic hardships of various sorts, and of the direction in which American capitalism seemed to be going. Some of the Settlement Houses, homes for the poor, were organized by Social Gospelers.[5] However, while there were some good motives and effects, it is worth considering the faddish quality of the Social Gospel movement. It focused so much on the problems of alleviating suffering that it lost the forest for the trees. When the First World War broke out, along with many other social reforms and utopian movements, the Social Gospelers were left staggered. How could the world have grown worse after such brilliant intellectual work (by various modern philosophers, artists, and movements) or after such effort? After the First World

5. It is worth noting here that one of the most famous of the Settlement Houses, Hull House, was run for decades by Jane Addams, a woman who made no secret of her lack of religion. See, Addams, *Twenty Years at Hull-House*, 1999.

War, the Social Gospel underwent an amazing transformation. Some associated with the movement developed methods of tracking people, so as to track poverty, and those new techniques found their way into new intellectual fields. Indeed, it has been suggested that the Social Gospel movement was the parent of the very modern, and typically atheistic, discipline of sociology.[6] Social moved ahead, leaving the gospel behind.

There are many questions we may ask regarding the example of the Social Gospelers, but what is clear is this: A specific gospel interpretation was interpreted again and presented as a new teaching. It offered a better society to bring in the millennium, and the new teaching led to new techniques, and none of it ended up where adherents might have wished.[7]

Prophecy Fads!

What is being claimed when Christians are urged to seek such-and-such a "blessing" from this place, or to travel over "there" to get the Spirit, or to hear and obey prophecies made by church leaders? Surely, no believer would wish to stifle the Spirit in whatever he chooses to do, and surely, God is capable of manifesting himself in any manner he desires and of pouring out the Spirit this way or that way. Equally surely, it appears that prophetic claims, outpourings of the Spirit, often take on the status of fads.

---

6. There are many sources for the history of the Social Gospel movement. A few we recommend are: Bateman, "Social Gospel and the Progressive Era"; Battle, "Brief History of the Social Gospel," 5–11; Ahlstrom, *Religious History of the American People*, or writings from one of the proponents at the time, Walter Rauschenbusch.

7. In case you are wondering where conservative Christians were in all of this, as it turns out, they were watching, unimpressed with what liberal Christians were attempting. Writes Greek: "[N]ot only did the Fundamentalist debate succeed in lessening the influence of liberal theology, it also spelled the end for most Protestant involvement in social concerns for the next forty years. Theological conservatives shunned social involvement as 'the poison of the social gospelers.'" Greek, *Religious Roots of American Sociology*, 201. We believe that the disconnect from society lasted a lot longer than forty years.

In the late 80s, the Kansas City Prophets, a name attached to them by some critics, promoted the Apostolic-Prophetic movement in parts of the Charismatic Church. The group associated with them "argued that God was spearheading a new revival from their churches, and that he was restoring the office of prophet."[8] But their prophecies struggled with, you know, actually being true.

In 1994 at a Vineyard church in Toronto, something happened. Ultimately growing worldwide, the Toronto Blessing featured ecstatic shouting, roaring (sometimes like lions), teeth being miraculously filled with gold fillings, healings, and holy laughter. There was lots and lots of laughter. A different and larger revival in Brownsville, Florida, began around 1995 and seems to have included supernatural healings and cures from drug-addiction. According to some news accounts, the size and numbers of the revival have been disputed. Lots of former members now attend other denomination churches, and the Brownsville Assembly of God church, where it started, wound up eleven-million dollars in debt. There is not as much laughing as there used to be.

Non-Traditional-Church Fads!

Naturally, claiming special workings of the Spirit or of new prophetic gifts is not the only way churches can distinguish themselves. Churches of every stripe have adopted all sorts of changes in attempts to, well, we often aren't quite sure what is being attempted. In 1972, Gene Getz took a shot at continuing orthodoxy and seeking contemporary relevance and the Fellowship Bible Church movement began.[9] In an attempt to be more relevant, Getz introduced sitting on stool with an overhead projector at

8. Alnor, *Heaven Can't Wait*, 24. Alnor states that some of the prophecies actually did not come true. He quotes one of the leaders admitting this was the case, but "mature" prophets had an accuracy rating approaching 85–95 percent.

9. We applaud Getz's efforts and think he did some things right. The FBC model continues in the Dallas area and has grown nationwide. What is always worth questioning (assuming what is proposed maintains orthodoxy) is: What is meant by "relevant"?

his side. Many churches began using something similar. Pulpits, thought to disconnect preachers from the congregation, were removed, the "Holy Desk" thought passé. Other structures unlike the traditional church began about the same time. House churches were revived as well as cell church movements. Then the cat was out of the bag, and new motivations for how churches might be structured and organized took over.

Purpose-Driven-Seeker-Friendly Fads!

Maybe one of the most influential fads, or at least, the most far reaching, in recent memory, is the change towards "seeker friendly" churches:

> At Saddleback Church we've . . . tried to recognize the waves God was sending our way, and we've learned to catch them. We've learned to use the right equipment to ride those waves, and we've learned the importance of balance. We've also learned to get off dying waves whenever we sensed God wanted to do something new. The amazing thing is this: The more skilled we become in riding waves of growth, the more God sends![10]

The "Willow Creek" model was suddenly, almost overnight, it seems, the model *du jour* for evangelicals. The goal was to reach those who avoided church, the Unchurched. How would they get pulled in? Why, with more programs, lots more, and attractive ones! No more boring old-fashioned church services with hymns and a twenty-five minute sermon! And this changed everything. Programs sprang up for families that had previously avoided church. Worships services brought in livelier music, casual dress on stage (and it was now a stage and no longer a pulpit), and dramatic presentations. Efficiency in showmanship and "liking" was given priority over formality.[11] And someone thought it a good idea to install smoke machines.

10. Warren, *Purpose Driven Church*, 14.
11. Willow Creek is the church outside Chicago that was one of the

Church-Organizational Fads!

Church Captains: when one person is assigned as the leader of a local body. Typically this is the pastor. Perhaps the oldest fad in the Church, the idea of a single spiritual leader in a congregation springs, of course, from the early Roman Church, and that path led to what became ultimately the Church, and then, in part because of this notion of priests as a separate category, became the Catholic Church. One of the ironies of the entire history since the Reformation, as we see it, is that many Protestant groups have either kept a regulated sort of priesthood, through massive denominational organizations, or have rejected anything like priests but have kept with leadership in one person. We bring this up as an example, perhaps THE example, of a long, historic, and utterly entrenched fad. Can anyone point to a single verse in the New Testament that supports the notion of a single man in charge of a congregation? We read that it is the responsibility of the elders of the church, a group, and that none of them had, or has, a monopoly on the truth; nor, we think it prudent to add, power (1 Tim 5:18; 1 Cor 9:9; Rom 4:4; Luke 10:7).

Consider what the employment situation is for many pastors. They are employees of either the local congregation or the diocese (or an equivalent). And what does this mean for hiring and firing? Who gets to decide? For the modern West, the pastor has become rather just another employee and the church structure is founded upon business models. There is a board made of up individuals who, maybe, have no understanding of either business or the Bible, but they get to determine the fate of the congregation as well as the careers (for we have made them such) of the pastors they hire. Did anyone stop to question how this might function? What problems could arise when a secular business model is applied as a means for Church structure?

---

originators of the movement and had a decades-long influence. To their credit, the leadership at Willow Creek reflected on some mistakes. Around 2007, they published a retraction, so to speak, apologizing for what they had done to their own congregation. For example, see, Hawkins and Parkinson, *Reveal*. For information on the retraction, see "Willow Creek Repents," and Branaugh, "Willow Creek's 'Huge Shift." Many other websites comment on the pros and more, the cons, of the movement.

23% More Spiritual!

Bus Fads!

For many years, there existed the strange phenomena of Bussing children to Sunday School. Some churches had fleets of buses. They started to buy old, used school busses and drove everywhere to pick up kids and adults alike for services. Church busses driving about everywhere, into ANOTHER church's territory, were ubiquitous on Sunday mornings.

Fads in Print!

It is possible that the marketing drive that became Christian publishing began early in the twentieth century with the publication of the Twelve-Step Program.[12] After the publication of this first "self-help" book, Christians jumped on board and started to churn out helpful books. Whereas previously, people would seek advice and counsel from a priest, pastor, or elder, now they could simply purchase a book. Clearly, there are meaningful and useful and enriching books out there, we have all benefitted from them, but many of what line the shelves of bookstores claim something like, "Begin this (insert activity) that will (insert positive term) your spiritual life/relationships/business!"

Just a brief listing of some of the big themes and titles reveals what fads in publishing have come and gone: endless titles on the end-times, trends in publishing themes surrounding Irish saints/ Celtic Christianity (whatever that means), books on angels, Old Testament saints, Romance novels derived from Old Testament themes and stories, the *Left Behind* series, Christian diet books, anything that includes the name C.S. Lewis in the title, and then perhaps the Queen Mother of all the fad books, *The Prayer of Jabez* by Bruce Wilkerson. Bruce's small tome, published in the nineties, took liberties with the prayer mentioned in First Chronicles 4, took liberties with later New Testament teachings on the temptations and problems of wealth, and took liberties with common sense. That didn't stop it from flying off the shelves, nor did it stop

12. Published in 1939, the book was entitled, *Alcoholics Anonymous*.

the production of spin-off products like *The Prayer of Jabez: Bible Study, The Prayer of Jabez: Devotional, The Prayer of Jabez: Expanding Your Boarders, The Prayer of Jabez Journal, The Prayer of Jabez for Kids, The Prayer of Jabez for Teens,* and Prayer of Jabez Cards (whatever those are), all written by Bruce Wilkerson. Thoughtfully, Mrs. Wilkerson was pulled into the business and wrote, *The Prayer of Jabez for Women.*

Varieties-of-Worship Fads!

With great trepidation, restraint, and just a bit of nausea, we address the fads wrapped up in the music conflicts of the past forty years. This seems to be one fad that has touched more Christians of various backgrounds than any other. When the Catholic church has nuns playing contemporary worships songs on guitars while swaying to the beat, well, you know the effect has been profound.

Some of the changes sprang up during the early 70s at places like Calvary Chapel, and with groups like Love Song. It appears that during the start of moving away from only classic hymns, there was resistance. Congregants were not interested in inconsequential ditties and preferred more serious music and lyrics. In an attempt to create such, Ray Stedman of Peninsula Bible Church, and musician John Fischer, sought teaching music, that is, songs that attempted to be teaching oriented. Indeed, it would be hard to think of Fischer's, "Have you Seen Jesus My Lord?" as anything but meaningful. What happened is that the shift to making music to please our ears led to the business of selling music to please our ears. Obviously that sort of business had been operating for years, but now a new genre was born: Christian Contemporary Music. And, of course, we all know that as soon as profit becomes a motive, all the arts, including music, increase in quality, with more thought to how the music will please Jesus and little given to marketing and money. Sigh.

During the 80s, one author asked a good question but then missed the boat: "Is the music a ministry, or is it entertainment? The motives, on both sides, were nearly always sincere and well-intentioned, rarely malicious."[13] Right, well-intentioned. We are reminded of the quote credited to Ray about the road to hell.

The music wars did not happen overnight, and for no reason. There were other changes in church worship taking place. We are persuaded that a variety of changes, many in an attempt to "update" or "contemporize" church worship, continued to develop a consumer mentality and a misunderstanding regarding music and perhaps church services entirely. Formality and boredom were out, informality and excitement were in. In a relatively short amount of time, churches went from robe-wearing worship leaders (and choirs) up on a platform behind an altar or altar table to no robes and no choirs, to essentially a pop band performing with lights and lots of microphones. Pastors, too, went from formal gowns to suits and ties to no ties and then to polo shirts; and whereas they used to stand behind a symbol of the seriousness of their station, the pulpit (formerly massive, sculpted, symbolic structures), now they come down to the level of the audience (formerly the congregation) and wear a microphone on their head, walk back and forth, and attempt to "relate" to the audience, much as, say, a stand-up comedian does. It is not only the worship teams and pastors who informalized the service, however. We remember being shushed as children for talking too loudly in the sanctuary (remember when they were called that?), and not being permitted to run about. Now during services, congregants walk in at all times, dressed in ways that would have scandalized their grandmothers, check their messages on their phones, and slurp bad church coffee while awaiting entertainment—sorry, we mean, while waiting to be spiritually enriched.

Church-Building-and-Use Fads!

And this led to all sort of changes in the fabric of the church itself. Hard to believe it took several centuries for our Christian ancestors to actually build a building dedicated to worship, then several

13. Baker, *Contemporary Christian Music,* 133. The author is indebted to the writers of the wiki page on contemporary Christian music for this citation.

more centuries to think about putting any kind of seating inside.[14] Up to the early twentieth century, churches still tended to be quite traditional in shape and function: rectangular design, with pews in rows, entrance at one end, and altar and pulpit on the other end toward which all faced. Then in relatively short order, churches began to change, first with the consideration of the sanctuary less as a place of worship and more as a place of teaching,[15] then followed new building techniques, new ways to make buildings comfortable, and then in the 60s, all had to change, and then in the 70s, all was made ugly, and then Willow Creek.

These changes transmogrified the spaces in myriad ways. Pews were removed in favor of moveable seating on carpeted floors, pulpits and platforms were moved about for clarity of seeing and hearing by the audience, and technology like overhead projectors was installed. Foyer spaces, previously for the transition from the world to the sanctuary (and for screaming babies) have become social spaces for increasingly better coffee, snacks, and perhaps the sale of various (Christian) books. And then there are the other facilities, most notably those with the dubious moniker, "Christian Life Center." These sprang up in response to, well, actually, we have no clue what may have motivated churches to spend millions of dollars on gymnasiums, bowling alleys, roller rinks, and other recreational centers; we assume it was from a desire to protect their children from the nasty non-Christian children.

All the fun changes noted above now get to take place in architectural structures that are often bad. We are not sure of the exact date when church design went to the dogs, but a good early example is from a famous modernist architect, Marcel Breuer,.[16]

---

14. Pews were put in, in some version, as early as the thirteenth century in England. After that, subscribed church "pew boxes" began to appear, paid for and frequently named for a family, wherein they would sit, every week. The closer to the pulpit, the more expensive the box.

15. For a good history of this part of the change see, Kilde, *When Church Became Theatre.*

16. Some architectural historians could point to earlier, indeed much earlier, controversies in church design. One that may strike contemporary readers is when churches in nineteenth-century London began, for economic reasons,

In the 50s, he was hired by the Benedictine sisters to start work on what would become the University of St. Mary in Bismarck, North Dakota. The chapel there is ahistorical in design, anticipating the 60s concrete Brutalist style. We feel confident that the design of the chapel functions as a means of keeping the locals warm. So hideous is its appearance, and indeed, meaning, that is must surely stoke the ire of anyone who has to endure being near it.[17] Bizarrely, there are many denominations that seem to have given up on anything like architectural meaning, or tradition, or even the most rudimentary taste, when building churches, and yet many of those same structures contain vast interior spaces dedicated to all sorts of classrooms, nurseries, kitchens, play area, social areas, and filled with sophisticated technology.

As with all the other fads mentioned here, the point is not that churches need to spend a certain amount on what they build, or that there is only one way to build; rather, it is to encourage thoughtfulness. For example, how frequently do church boards seek to build a church with design that actually means something connected to the history of church buildings and Christianity as opposed to some current trend that will make the church appear *avant garde*?

---

to use brick as a building material. This was thought vulgar and inappropriate for a house of worship. Of course, we could take things right back to the beginning and ask: Who ever thought Christians were *supposed* to be building large buildings?

17. The meaning of Breuer's work is clearly antithetical to anything to do with the Christian faith, or any other faith. Breuer was a product of the Bauhaus, a design development that spread, somewhat like a fungus, from Germany to most of Europe and America, as well as the Soviet-block nations, weirdly. Among the goals are a purity of functionalism and a distain for tradition. Inspiring the architectural designers of this movement was the 1911 dull, glass box Fagus Shoe Factory. We find it astonishing that the sisters and their bishop in North Dakota never stopped to consider more carefully what it is that Breuer's architecture means.

Impending-End Fad!

Sometime in the 60s when, you know, lots of things got crazy, some Christians decided that it was time to really get into the study of the End Times. It did not much matter that both Paul and John wrote that Jesus would return as a thief in the night, and that the word "rapture" does not appear in Scripture; still, we needed to *figure this out*! Dallas Theological Seminary honed in on Rapture studies, and this was followed by an amazing bit of publishing success in 1970, *The Late Great Planet Earth*, by Hal Lindsey (who attended DTS for one of his degrees). And a fad was born!

In addition to other books by Lindsey, there were the execrable films like, *Thief in the Night*, and the Chick Tracts, little publications books that were designed to terrify people into loving Jesus. There were terrific bumper stickers like, "In case of Rapture, this car will self-destruct." Ah, the 70s were good times. All the fun of the Rapture and leisure suits! Like with our other fads, did we not stop to consider how much vanity is wrapped up in thinking our generation is the "last generation," or even how the goals of our life, or the goals of our church, would be different if we knew Christ would not return for another thousand years? No, we all plowed in and imagined that any second, half of all people (us, not that other half), would disappear, showing those unbelievers what-for.

Counseling Fads!

Of course, one of the most obvious ways that fads start for Christians is when they embrace some version of a fad in the secular world. Or, when they react and turn in the opposite direction of the secular world. Nothetic Counseling, or Confrontative Biblical Counseling (or other names), began with the publication of, *Competent to Counsel*, in 1970, penned by Jay E. Adams. The method is an attempt to counsel biblically, and an attempt to reject secular therapy that is not biblically guided. Part of what it featured was the counselor telling the patient how they ought to act based on what the Bible teaches and not merely listening to them and seeking some inner motivations for their behaviors. Some proponents think that psychology is not enough, that it required biblical guidance and teaching first. Other Christian therapists suggest that if someone is clearly psychologically ill, they need to be brought to a place where they are *able* to hear what Scripture says. We cite this example, not because we know anything about the practice of psychology, but because it demonstrates something about the way fads originate: they can spring up out of perhaps a-less-than-rigorous consideration of the needs and outcomes they may address.

We-Promise-a-Million Fads!

Remember the Promise Keepers and their massive rallies? It was estimated that 800,000 attended the Stand in the Gap Rally in DC in 1997. A football coach from Colorado started the program and promised, at that 1997 rally, that in the year 2000, Promise Keepers would sponsor rallies at every state capital in the US with speakers talking about all the racial reconciliation that they have done. Coach McCarthy proclaimed, "They are going to be able to say, 'Yes, we teach, preach, model and live racial reconciliation.' And when that happens, the church of Jesus Christ is going to be able to stand up and say we can testify that the giant of racism is dead inside the church of Jesus Christ."[18] So, how did that work out for them? By 1999, the organization seemed to be tapped for funds and after that had a hard time generating the kinds of attendance numbers at conferences previously had. Fair calling this a fad? It was new, generated lots of excitement, made lots of promises (which was good for an organization with that name), and then, safe to say, fizzled.[19]

18. This quote is found in most online sources that covered the rally on October 4, 1997. The six-hour rally can be viewed on C-Span's website.

19. See, Bartkowski, *Whatever Happened to the Promise Keepers?* Bartkowski makes this worthy observation: "Thus, PK's anti-establishment approach to faith was its greatest strength and its most glaring weakness. PK was catapulted into the limelight and attracted men by the thousands through [sic] because it gave a free-flowing character to spirituality. In this way, it successfully dressed up religion in garb, such as sport, that is very familiar to

McMission Fads!

You know these: when someone at church solicits funds for a week long "mission's trip." These are fun! They often feature high school or college students going to another country, one they have never visited, one for which they do not know the language, to "minister" to the locals. Maybe an important project is included, like painting the walls of some building or performing puppet shows. The best part is when the emotional young people return and are asked to share their experiences with the church. Tears are shed, eyes opened, and everyone gets to feel good about what they have accomplished in the name of Jesus. I hope it goes without saying that exposing students to other cultures, having them experience the world, are valuable activities to teach them things beyond their immediate life. If mission's trips were sold as this, and did not solicit funds in the name of Jesus, it would make more sense. As they are typically pitched, McMissions just cause us to flat-out worry about where some Christians minds are at and how much more patience we can ask of God.

Beating-Your-Children Fad!

Anyone raised in an evangelical church in the 70s will know the name of Bill Gotthard and his Institute of Basic Youth Conflicts. This was perhaps the fad of all fads in that it was hugely popular, widely praised, accrued enormous funds, and ended in disgrace. Parents would attend huge conferences for days, receive big red binders filled with papers, and were taught fascinating authority principles, like: God, then man, then the woman. Some people attended every year. They learned that even more important than their Christian ministry was their family. And Gotthard taught lots about families,

---

American men. But this quality also meant that its fame would not last very long, as is commonly the case with revivalistic movements designed to attract a limited constituency (in this case, men)." Bartkowski, *Whatever Happened to the Promise Keepers?*, . In other words, it was a fad. This and other thoughtful excerpts from Bartkowski's book can be found online at the Hartford Institute for Religion Research.

such as that children needed to be spanked frequently. After attending the conferences, many parents would go out and purchase a wooden rod specifically for spanking purposes. And he also taught about marriage relationships and how to keep them alive. For example, that wives ought to meet their husbands at the door after work, dressed in vinyl, and with a seductive glass of orange juice at the ready. Of course, as these things go, word got out that Gotthard never married and never had kids, and that took some of the gloss off of his teachings. Even more things got out in 2014, when 34 women accused him of sexual harassment. In 2016, a group of them sued Gotthard and his organization.[20] Perhaps too many women walked into the workplace holding glasses of orange juice?

What-Wristband-Would-Jesus-Wear Fad!

In 1896, Charled Sheldon published the bestseller, *In His Steps: What Would Jesus Do?* In the 1990s, that subtitle could be seen cuffed in abbreviated form on thousands of Christian wrists. WWJD exploded into 90s American culture in that way that only really awful Christian fads can explode. Suddenly everyone, it seemed, was sporting a rubbery wristband with WWJD on it. Of course, as fads go and money starts to flow, more products were produced: WWJD appeared on nearly any item imaginable. In classic fad manner, it spread, caught national attention, became marketable, became fashionable, as lots of kids who did not know what the letters WWJD even stood for wore the wristbands, and then it was gone.

Not-Dating Fads!

In the 90s, Joshua Harris wrote *I Kissed Dating Goodbye*, an attempt to bring a kind of sexual purity and a better understanding

---

20. The suit did not go ahead. Other details emerged to discredit Gotthard, such as that he earned a PhD from the unaccredited Louisiana Baptist University, and that he thought Cabbage Patch dolls were idolatrous.

of courtship to evangelical adolescents. It made a splash, sold nearly a million copies, and inspired youth-group leaders to change what they had taught. We think he was correct in how out-of-line dating has grown, but was this, some New Thing, the way to go about teaching students to live faithful lives? Tragically, it has all the hallmarks of a fad: grew quickly in popularity, changed the way things were done at church, messed up a few lives (specifically, those who were not "pure" and thought they had no hope of becoming so), and ended with, once again, a daft story on the part of the person from whom it originated: in 2019 Harris renounced his Christian faith and apologized to homosexuals because of the "culture of exclusion and bigotry" to which he thought his work had contributed.

Essential Fads!

You know who they are. You can often tell they are at church even before you can see them, especially if they have young kids who are ill: you can smell them. They carry those black cases with tiny vials of essential oils. And then, not always, but frequently, they attempt to sell those vials to their brothers and sisters at church. Mostly these oils seem to be essential for annoying other people.

Patriarchy Fad!

Vision Forum, founded in 1998, promoted Old Testament teachings about patriarchy, of men having proper roles as husbands and fathers.[21] This seems an odd fad, as they were not claiming that men were to lord it over women, but were, it appears, teaching

21. This is no to be confused with the John Eldredge masculinity fad as outlined in his 2001 book, *Wild at Heart*; nor his 2011, *Wild at Heart Revised and Updated*, nor any of these other titles: *Wild at Heart Field Manual, Wild at Heart: A Band of Brothers Small Group Participant's Guide, Wild at Heart Facilitator's Guide, Wild at Heart Video Discussions, Wild at Heart Journal, Wild at Heart: A Band of Brothers Small Group Video,* and the one for ladies, *Captivating: A Guided Journal to Aid in Unveiling the Mystery of a Woman's Soul.*

biblical leadership. But then, why was it called the Patriarchy Movement? Alas, President Doug Phillips's understanding about patriarchy was rather poorly expressed in 2013, when he confessed to infidelity and the ministry subsequently closed down.

Hillsong Fad!

No. Just, no.

Pseudo-Jew Fad!

This is the strange phenomena of Christians adopting the practices of Jewish rituals and customs. They are not former Jews, they are not Messianic Jews (who tend to actually be ethnically Jewish), nor are they the (seeming) non-Christians referred to by some as "Torah-Observant Gentiles."[22] No, these folks are evangelicals who, for perhaps a number of reasons, desire to study and practice Judaic rules and traditions. At least one source refers to the practice as Philosemitism.[23] We prefer the term, Pseudo-Jew and suggest this has all the hallmarks of a fad: These are esoteric practices that most evangelicals, perhaps most Christians, do not practice and do not know about, but they add a touch of mysticism, they add ritual (which many evangelicals assiduously avoid, except not), they are exclusive ("Oh, we can't make the Bible study, we're having Seder!"), and they portend to offer some kind of insight/wisdom/ richness that "regular" Christianity does not. Thus it has, of course, more than a whiff of Gnostic exclusivity and vanity: "I am in and have this understanding," it says, "and you do not." Also like most fads, when you examine them more closely, they just don't make that much sense. Really, if we are in a post-law time of the faith, which has been the case since, ah, well, the time of Christ (or at the latest, Acts 10), then how does it make sense to go *back* to the

22. For a bit more detail on this last group, see Kaiser, "For Some Believers Trying to Connect with Jesus, the Answer Is to Live Like a Jew."

23. Hobson, "Evangelicals Turning to Jewish Customs?."

ritual law? Sure, read up on it, study it, maybe go to some Jewish services and a Seder if you get invited, but to incorporate this into your Christian walk? After Acts 10, do any Christians seriously think that not eating pork will do *anything* for their faith?

Fad-We-Are-Not-Sure-What-to-Call-So-We'll-Call-It-the-Hipster Fad!

Something about Christian practice seems to have grown more, well, cool. Perhaps this is the remaining vestiges of the Seeker Movement, wherein churches attempted to cool-ify? The attempt to make churches more appealing (whatever that means), sought those who were turned off by church (whatever that means), and attempted to bring them back. Our evidence for this change is seen in the casualification of Sunday morning services, the proliferation of hipsters performing on stage, more visibility of fashion statements, and more attention to hipster physical appearances, like piercings, tattoos, and unusual beards. (Hm, although the latter might indicate a Pseudo-Jew.) It seems to us that it is yet another step in a direction without much thought. Does being hip bring us closer to Jesus, increase our devotion and care, or help us make disciples? Might it instead be about comfort with the world, avoiding standing out, and dodging conflict?

Mess-with-the-Names-Church Fad!

Chartres Cathedral outside Paris does not have a large illuminated sign indicating its name. Lots of changes have taken place in church names. Some drop any mention of their denominational affiliation, others are hip. Names and phrases attempt to connect more with potential visitors. Using terms such as "real" or "relevant" to describe your church—this is a growing fad. Most seeker churches now put this in their title or church description somewhere: "Here at [insert church name], we are real and relevant."[24]

24. See "Ever-Changing Fads of the Church." The unnamed author of this

Shiplap-Everywhere Fad!

If your church is as good as the one we attend, then you will have the joy of seeing, up behind the platform, worn wooden horizontal panels as wall decoration. Shiplap! The panels are perhaps illuminated with clever floor lights that could throw up changing and generally repellent colors of light upon the walls. If you are lucky, there are some Edison bulbs nearby for extra spirituality! Why do churches do this? To make church pretty? A few months later, one of us was abroad and stumbled into a coffee shop located inside of a historic (and still active) church. There, in the hipster sanctuary (if we can use that word about this space), were the exact same kinds of walls with the exact same kind of illumination (if we can use that word about this space). A friend suggested maybe they were watching, "Total Sanctuary Makeover."

Swisstianity Fads!

We started this chapter with an example of a fad from the nineteenth century, the Social Gospel Movement—a fad that spun out in directions unexpected and less than helpful for Christians. We end this section with a much more recent fad, one lurking at the back of so many recent movements in evangelical churches. We prefer to call this position, "Swisstianity." A useful term, for not only does it attempt a kind of neutrality, but it also posits (if that is the right word for the vague thinking) a position full of holes. (See also, "Inanity.") It works something like this: in an effort to appear non-dogmatic, to seem generous, giving, open, emergent (as in, emerging from that to this, or out of something into something else), pluralistic, diverse, tolerant, and *nice*, Christians need to stop seeking answers. All our answers are, at the end of the day, distilled through our class, race, and gender filters. We all are filled with sin, and we all skew any answers about God to our own benefit (and typically to the detriment of those other groups of Christians).

---

site also points to catchy names of sermons and notices on signs, and then he adds: "This is the latest fad along with the emergent church." We like him.

Instead of seeking answers, an obsession with the Greco-Roman Western intellectual tradition (a tradition known to be sexist, bigoted, homophobic, racist, etc.), we need to *just experience*. You know, real life. One critic, in discussing how new terms are bandied about, such as "real" and "relevant" mentioned above, writes:

> Now I'm all for being a real disciple of Jesus and relevant in the sense that I live in this world and I have a short time to preach the gospel to the lost, but they use the term to mean that they will avoid anything that might offend you, embarrass you, and will avoid trying to teach you the hypostatic union of Jesus Christ but will instead offer answers for real life.[25]

Squishy as Swisstianity is, it can be found in a variety of Christian places from the Emergent Church movements of the past twenty years to the increasing liberalization of many Christian groups to pretty much anything written by Rob Bell. It portends to be less dogmatic and that means, of course, it is a more comfortable fit with the world. What the church needs to offer, some suggest, is love and wonder. We need to let go of our "silly answers" and just be accepting. It is more about the journey than the destination! The Bible is a story, not a book of rules! Who are we to judge? Who am I to judge? We ought to each seek to be honest with our own convictions![26]

Summary

Churches, as groups of people, worshippers, organizations, and physical structures, have gone through seeming paroxysms of change during the twentieth century (mostly, it appears, during the 70s). We discover that Christians seem to endlessly repeat

25. See "The Ever Changing Fads of the Church."

26. The most recent example of this fad can be found, we believe, in Rob Bell's most recent book, *What Is the Bible Anyway?* Church elders used to call what this book teaches heresy, a term not much in favor today. But surely heresy may be described as just your opinion about doctrine? A response to this way of thinking is offered in the next chapter.

techniques, quarrels, objects, and methods. Isn't the definition of insanity repeating the same offense and expecting a different result? It does not appear we have quite learned much of anything.

It is fair at this point for the reader to ask: Why does it matter? We have fads in the culture. Things move on, each generation has its own struggles, interests, and goals, so it is perfectly right that each period be looked back upon with a bit of a grin by later generations. Sure, 100-percent polyester leisure suits were thought to be the cutting edge of fashion back in the 70s, but now we want our own look, our own way, our own expression. Can't each generation sort out their own fads? Isn't that merely how generations work, how we keep current? What is the problem?

". . . I will bring you to the land not of questions but of answers, and you shall see the face of God."

"Ah, but we must all interpret those beautiful words in our own way! For me there is no such thing as a final answer. The free wind of inquiry must *always* continue to blow through the mind, must it not? 'Prove all things'. . . to travel hopefully is better than to arrive."

"If that were true, and known to be true, how could anyone travel hopefully? There would be nothing to hope for."

"But you must feel yourself that there is something stifling about the idea of finality? Stagnation, my dear boy, what is more soul-destroying than stagnation?"

"You think that, because hitherto you have experienced truth only with the abstract intellect. I will bring you where you can taste it like honey and be embraced by it as by a bridegroom.
Your thirst shall be quenched."

—C.S. LEWIS, *THE GREAT DIVORCE*

... stay there in Ephesus so that you may command certain people not to teach false doctrines any longer, or to devote themselves to myths and endless genealogies. Such things promote controversial speculations rather than advancing God's work-which is by faith. The goal of this command is love, which comes from a pure heart and a good conscience and a sincere faith. Some have departed from these and have turned to meaningless talk. They want to be teachers of the law, but they do not know what they are talking about or what they so confidently affirm. We know that the law is good if one uses it properly. We also know that the law is made not for the righteous but for lawbreakers and rebels, the ungodly and sinful, the unholy and irreligious, for those who kill their fathers or mothers, for murder-ers, for the sexually immoral, for those practicing homosexuality, for slave traders and liars and perjurers-and for whatever else is contrary to the sound doctrine that conforms to the gospel concerning the glory of the blessed God ...

—FIRST TIMOTHY 1: 3–11

3

The Fad and Why It Is a Problem

"This time it's different" are the four
most dangerous words in the English language.

—MARC BELLEMARE[1]

A dog returns to its vomit.

—SECOND PETER 2:22

ONE OF THE GOALS of the previous chapter was to make clear this troubling fact: Christians have bought into the Culture of Fad. The fad is a problem for Christians, if not for all humans.[2] Some of the examples from the previous chapter speak for themselves: they show what are frequently stupid manifestations of bad ideas

---

1. Bellemare, "Chronocentrism: 'This Time It's Different.'"

2. The pursuit of fads is not good for anyone, Christian or otherwise. Trendy superficiality is just as dumb for humans who do not follow Christ. One example that has wrecked shocking destruction on a vast number of cities and lives are popular trends in architecture. Historic neighborhoods and buildings have been decimated to make room for the new, the better, the more efficient. What it produced is urban blight, sometimes more expensive to maintain buildings, and almost without exception, sheer ugliness.

applied to the Christian faith. There are many reasons why fads are a problem. Ultimately, the effect is one of superficiality, a dilution of the faith. Symptoms include spiritual weakness, the fading of any kind of meaningful contribution that Christianity might make to either the culture or to individual humans, and the reduction of Christianity to just another choice in a world filled with lots of superficial choices. The world does not want our fads, it has plenty of its own that are more visceral and more aesthetically satisfying. Christians, and Christianity, are supposed to be offering the world hope, an eternal and unchanging savior, upon which all meaning can be affixed. But, alas, we all too frequently opt for the fad.

Fad?

What is meant by the word "fad"? It might help to have a look at the opposite of a fad, a fad's antithesis. Antonyms for fad are terms like: calm, boredom, and tradition. Excepting the last term, classic (a discussion of that is below), who wants any of those? Sounds terrible. We much prefer the synonyms for fad: craze, passion, last word [ha!], sensation, and style! All that is exciting and seductive. But other synonyms are less desirable and point to some of the problems: obsession, fetish, fixation.

Origins for the term "fad" are not agreed upon. It may have come from nineteenth-century English terms: *fiddle-faddle—fid-fad*—fad.[3] One dictionary source from 1824 suggests *faddy*, also drawn from *fiddle-faddle*. *Fadaise*, French for "trifle, nonsense," is ultimately drawn from the Latin *fatuus*, "stupid" (from which we derive "fatuous"). This same source finds a root from a word in an 1881 text for "fashion, craze." The Century Dictionary defines "fad" as "trivial fancy adopted and pursued for a time with irrational zeal."[4] When stated bluntly like the above terms, it seems obvious that fads ought not be connected to Christianity. What is there about the faith, about Christ the Rock, God the Perfect and

---

3. The OED suggests this origin.
4. *Etymonline*, s.v. "fad."

Immutable, that would push us to adopt a "trivial fancy"?[5] And if we do so, what problems does that create?

How Christians Think about Fads

In short, we don't. Mark Noll's insightful 1994 book, *The Scandal of the Evangelical Mind*, opens with what has become a well-known phrase: "The scandal of the evangelical mind is that there is not much of an evangelical mind."[6] Similarly, we make the claim that one of the scandals of church fads is that few stop to consider them. There are historic reasons for that (discussed in the next chapter). Our contention is that fads are damaging in a myriad of ways to Christians individually and to the church as a whole. Fads, lacking substance, cheapen the message of the gospel and, lacking reflection, uglify the church.

Fads seem to seethe through the culture, ripping into anything in their way. How much of our lives are driven by fads? Clothes, interior design, electronics, shoes, cars, our vocabulary—how much of it means anything? We've got to aim for the next big thing, the newest, latest, but where is the qualitative concern? We've arrived at the ludicrous level of fad where we don't even consider the value, the evaluation, the qualitative matters—just the new. We don't even excuse our participation in fads in the name of productivity, health, or charity anymore. Even if what we are doing drains our budgets, even if it is killing us, we march on for the next thing, the next damn widget, the next Gnostic hope in finding some kind of purpose to our lives and confirming that we are a step ahead of everyone else. The problem is that we have bought into a worldly way of thinking and now it spills over into our faith.

5. Why some pursue fads is examined in chapter 4.

6 Noll, *Scandal of the Evangelical Mind*, 3.

The Emotional Appeal

This is a fundamental impetus for fads: they make us feel better. At least for a short while. We see or hear the ad for the New Thing, we hear others talk about it and its success, and then we jump in. That purchase, that adaptation, that *whatever* brings an emotional buzz. You got it! You are there/in/ahead/better/more spiritual! Congratulations. And we know how long that emotional feeling lasts. Actually, we know all about how feelings work, how they are associated with buying and obtaining, with the (temporary) satisfying of desires. Ever known anyone who "self-medicates" with constant purchasing? But is this a big problem? Why can't we have our small pleasures and just relax about them? Life is short, full of suffering and pain, so enjoy.

The problem with the emotional motivation is that it confuses spirituality with emotions. People go to church, hear music that pleases them, listen to a sermon that makes them feel some strong emotions, and chat with friends who make them feel warm and welcome. None of that is, of course, out of line. The problem is when they experience all those feelings of pleasure and then come home and think, "Wow, what a deeply spiritual time I've had at church." (We are persuaded that lots of this misunderstanding of church is what lies behind the various stylistic "wars" churches have suffered through.) Fads typically follow the same pattern: "Wow, this New Thing makes me feel this way! I'm more spiritual!" But what happens when the feelings fade? Does the spirituality linked with it also fade? Sure, because it was never about being more devout, obedient, or loving. It was about feelings.

But it is worse. If we seek an emotional response, it sets us up to fail. It is tragically common to see people marry based on romance and feelings. What happens if we attempt to build a marriage on mere romance? The feelings change, fade, cool off, and the spouses think perhaps the love is gone, or they never loved enough, or in the right way, and then often the marriage fails. By the same token, what if we buy the fad (participate in the seminar, go to the conference, read the book) and everyone around us is having emotional response, but you are not? Or perhaps you are not have *enough* feelings? The *wrong type* of feelings? Or if the feelings just do what feelings always do and quietly fade away? Is that because you are not sensitive/spiritual/committed enough?

Finally, the emotional path prevents us from going deeper. If deeper is associated with feelings, this has the effect of denigrating any rational or intellectual attempts to understand the faith, to grow. Those are more work, and that mightn't feel at all pleasant. In the end, the fad leads to superficiality. The superficial can persuade that we have arrived somewhere, at some level of maturity, insight and wisdom, when, in fact, we have not. The false is a substitute for the more substantial truth, for a more difficult wisdom. It can take us from the narrow path. Emotions can last a long time, and we can prop them up in different ways; they are a problem not at first, but only when you need real faith, when there is a crisis. Then where are the feelings, or more importantly, who cares about the feelings during a crisis? When you need genuine faith and a solid relationship with Christ, what use is happy/clappy, your WWJD wristband, and the Prayer of Jabez?

The emotional approach is related to other troubling issues. For example, our culture has deeply struggled with the separation of what is aesthetically pleasing, that is, gives pleasure, from that which is beautiful, that is, edifying. For at least the past century and a half, in the West, there has been an utter confusion in thinking that what is beautiful can only mean what a person prefers, what gives a person pleasure.[7] To fail to equate the beautiful with what is good leads to lots of screwy intellectual problems—like the confusion of emotional responses for spiritual growth.

What else gets lost? Where is there a place for reverence? Grief? Humility? Repentance? Some traditions do emphasize some of these more serious (and rarely fun or pleasurable) reflections as a routine part of their services. For example, some Presbyterian traditions have services that include a Scripture reading

7. In previous centuries, what was beautiful was equated with what was true and good and not with aesthetic responses. More on the history of this idea is in chapter 4.

over personal sin and our fallen state. This is not done to stimulate emotions (although it may do so). It is done to stimulate repentance and an awareness of who we actually are (and what Christ has actually done). But how many Christian denominational traditions do not consider these reverent, formal, and sobering reflections as part of their weekly services? Why not? Surely part of the reason must be that it is not popular to think about repentance and our sin nature. For at least the past decade, so many have been concerned about what sorts of thoughts and feelings are presented to potential visitors to church who might be turned off. We want church to be appealing. But sadly, and we all know this: the trivial can so easily be packaged in an attractive and pleasurable format. The superficial appears to be substantial, but is only skin deep.

Finally, we might also consider how entertainment plays a part. What is the difference between entertainment and other activities? It is to *entertain*. That is, it attempts to titillate, excite, thrill, and please. Often entertainment is associated with distraction. We immerse ourselves in TV binges, to "veg." Fine. Good. Relaxation is not a sin. But when entertainment becomes enmeshed with worship, with the Christian life, then the Christian life and church become associated with entertainment and we have the same problems mentioned above. Entertainment at church contains an important paradox: it is about my satisfaction in being entertained, and yet at the same time it focuses on the show, the actual entertaining part. Not a great leap of the intellect is required to see that neither of those aspects has anything to do with worshiping God. Worship may entertain, but its goal is to direct us back towards a proper relationship with God.

What do we do when church ceases to be entertaining? Part of the effort of the Seeker-Friendly fad was an attempt to tone down "serious" worship and bring in more contemporary music, casual dress, and dramatic readings: How is this not seeking to make a more entertaining worship service? Not to put too fine a point on it, but frankly, even when it is at its most entertaining, church ain't that great as entertainment. Are the unchurched rushing in to see live music? Probably not. Meanwhile, what might our children be learning? We had the privilege of judging an art show at a local megachurch. Among the people we met was a well-meaning mother who directed us to have a look at the Sunday School rooms. We went upstairs and entered a hallway the size of a small airport terminal. On either side were six rooms, each differently themed, each fantastically themed, one with fake jungle décor, another with a space ship interior, or medieval castle crenels, or Aladdin's Castle, and each with a puppet stage, audio-visual systems, props, everything. The mother later explained that those rooms were so important since "we're trying to keep our kids in church." Sure, but at the same time the kids are learning that church is all about entertainment. How many will leave the church when they begin to find Sunday mornings boring?

The emotional appeal is problematic for the reasons mentioned, but also because, fundamentally, it becomes an appeal to ME. Emotional appeals are generally about ME, MY desires and satisfactions, MY pursuits and dreams. Where is the self-sacrifice? Where is the pouring out, the fool for Jesus, and the narrow gate? Where, in short, is the pursuit of the transcendent truth and the hope for something beyond mere human desires, or knowledge, or wisdom? Where is the search for the objective? When the truth is lost, dismissed, forgotten, the subjective worm emerges and survives by constant emotional stimulation. Once loosed, it crawls into everything and affects all. Truth is lost, wisdom is reduced to opinion, beauty becomes pleasure, debate becomes shouting, might makes right, and all is reduced to manifestations of the will.

Pride and Vanity

What naturally follows the privileging of the will is pride and vanity. Whether Christian or non-believer, demanding our own way leads to dreadful consequences. Pride, as we say, comes before the fall. Christians are well aware that pride is a problem, so we keep an eye out for it; however, Screwtape is clever and vanity seeps in at every opportunity. When we recognize that humans can feel proud of their lack of pride, well, we know it is going to be a tough slog.

Unfortunately, many are the fads embraced by Christians that are driven by subtle, selfish, little strokes of pride; we feel the need to catch up, or keep up, in some way not spiritual or biblical. And when we do catch up, at least in our own estimation, then a sliver of superiority can take hold. One of the easiest ways to stroke our own superiority is to think we are a bit ahead of the other folks. Of course, Christians recognize that "keeping up with the Joneses" is a problem, sure, but we have our own ways to work around that.

How might this work in regard to the manifold books published each year by Christian publishers? Who garners the most interest when it comes to new books? Do we think more is written and said, that is, more faddish buzz generated, by someone writing a commentary on Matthew? Or by another Rob Bell bombshell? Or yet another book by Max Lucado? Christians are just as susceptible as anyone to the new, the cutting edge, the *avant guard*, the next-big-thing. And publishers want to print and then sell whatever it is that will sell. Exciting books sell more. One of the reasons they sell more is that a particular author may have a tremendous ministry, and actually be saying things that help us to grow. Another reason must surely be how the fad works: "Oh, you've not read the latest Beth Moore study?" When we've read something someone else has not read, well, that has the potential to just fluff our feathers a bit. If we are not careful, we can begin to imagine we have just a bit of a leg up on our peers because we've read more, or the latest, or have kept up with some author's tweets. This is a temptation for both the readers of whatever book but also the publishers who want to sell more books.

Notably, it can also run full circle when authors find themselves wanting to catch the next Big Thing. Imagine an ambitious writer pens a book that does have a new something to say on a particular issue. It is authentic, true, useful, filled with wisdom. It is picked up by a big press. They want to sell books so they begin to push hard to sell it. Good. Okay. But then they want him to pen a second book. Maybe the author does not have another idea ready, one that has been considered, shared, prayed over, one that fills him with peace. But the author has to come up with *something*.

Do some of these authors go off the rails? This problem is endemic to an entire system of how the world deals with fads. They want fads because they don't really have much of anything else. We don't want fads. We get fads shoved at us due to our embrace of the same network of systems that generate fads for the world.

The author Peter Rollins commented, publically and honestly, on issues of pride in publishing.[8] He said before his first book was published that he mused over the idea of not having his name on it. It may have been too much for his vanity, too much showing off. Then, when his first book came out, he held it in his hands and thought that perhaps the font was too small and maybe it would have been better if his name received a bit more attention. We liked his forthrightness and it made us consider: What happens if we wrote a book on the problem of fads that becomes a fad itself? It could grow into a divisive and snarky fad, to dismiss and denigrate other fads. The dismissal comes in the form of a quick look down the nose, "Well, yes, you would be into that as you do not know the latest fad is to not be into fads." What happens if this book, criticizing how Christians embrace stupid fads ends up becoming popular? It would mean lots of money and fame and assured godliness because everyone knows that the appropriate measure of quality and goodness and spirituality is how popular something is!

A final related warning to the fad in books and reading has to do with a sort of Neo-Gnosticism. Gnosticism refers to a heresy of the second century in which some thought they were privy to a special learning (and thus special exceptions) from God. We use it to refer to that faddish sort of thinking to which any of us can succumb: in thinking we know more, we have better knowledge than the next guy. The trouble with this thinking is it means whoever is in possession of (or, perhaps more accurately, possessed by) the latest fad is the superior being: "Now we know!" thinking belittles our ancestors, tradition, and history, and creates an appealing snobbery to the next generation.[9] Examples abound: our culture

8. Rollins, "Idolatry of God."

9. We find some of the Emergent thinking to be fueled with a kind of Gnostic appeal. For an insightful investigation of the issues, and a thoughtful

used to think that Sundays ought to be special and so businesses were closed, TV was off, cinema was avoided, *but now we know* those practices were just silly! Our great-grandparents thought Elvis shaking his hips on television to be too sexually provocative, *but now we know* that it was okay! Our forebears thought mixed-swimming to be a bad idea, *but now we know* it's not a problem! Particularly for anything having to do with sex, it does not take much observation to realize that perhaps grandmom and granddad may have been onto something.

Of course, it is not only in publishing where something can warp into a fad. Two other examples of pride and vanity are worth considering. The first is an aspect of hipster Christianity mentioned in chapter 2, and has to do with attractiveness. We all desire to be attractive. We know that can be a problem when WE are seeking to be the attractive element. We may ask: What happened to "fools for Jesus"? The reply is typically, "We want to be attractive to the world." We reply, "But Jesus said he would use the foolish things of the world." Right. So where does that leave us? If nothing else, we can be sure that if we are attractive to the world in the wrong way, then we ought to be suspicious. If we are attempting to attract the world, in the wrong way, then that ought to give us pause. And if the world applauds what we are doing, then we should increase our vigilance.

The other example is one that has plagued evangelicals perhaps since they split off from mainline denominations in the nineteenth century.[10] Evangelicals seemed to desire a sort of special revelation all the time. This is usually referred to as God's will. How much angst has been generated by evangelicals attempting to decide God's will for their lives? Surely, we know much of what God wills for us already, as spelled out in Scripture? Yet sometimes that seems not enough. What is it we hope for? We hope

---

response, see, Carson, *Becoming Conversant with the Emerging Church*.

10 If you are an evangelical, you should read up on the history. It did not fall from the sky fully formed but was a series of deliberate choices, as well as reactions, to cultural and scientific challenges. We recommend Mark Noll's book, mentioned earlier, *Scandal of the Evangelical Mind*. It covers some of the history as well as some of the problems.

for a special experience *just for me*, my own special knowledge, because I am special! Is it possible that we discover God's will more by study and discipline rather than a random flip through the Bible followed by a bolt of lightning?

There is an endpoint for all this pride. We will, after following this path, discover that it *really is* about our own experiences, that those are what *really* matter.[11] The fad feeds this, strokes us, sucks up to us. Read *this* and then *you* will have a better marriage/children/Christian life/more money. This is a prideful maneuver for Christians. Pride is a sin as it puts one, or something else, into the place of God. The fad works to have you decide, if nothing else, which fads are appropriate, which ought to be adopted, which are more spiritual and enlightening. We all need, and ought to desire, proper godly discernment, attempting to sort the trivial from the genuine, the wood, hay, and stubble from the gold. We know we all make mistakes and we see the results of foolishness, error, and sin in our own lives, but also culturally. So, the criteria for discernment is of the utmost importance. It is but a short step from following godly wisdom to a vain corruption leading to self-divinization.

Laziness and Silver Bullets

Consider the role of laziness in the destructive work of the fad. What is it exactly that makes some New Thing suddenly become a popular, hot commodity? Might it have to do the very American desire for the quick solution? Who wants to diet and exercise when we can just drink a bottle of this healthy whatever, or take a pill? Fads are sometimes about speed and efficiency. Faster, quicker, easier, cheaper: our Americanism spills over into every aspect of our lives. We don't want to wait for anything. We desire, as we all know, immediate gratification. We desire the quick fix, the silver bullet, the magic potion that will make all things simpler and ourselves slightly more attractive.

---

11. For more on this destructive topic, see this wise book: Carey, *Good News for Anxious Christians*, 175–90.

But what is the problem for Christians? It is the problem of big steps, little steps. It takes lots and lots of little steps to become a good violin player. It does not happen all at once. Fads often promise the quicker, faster, easier way. We do not seek simplicity and effortlessness in all areas of life. Athletes, bankers, doctors, mechanics, all are expected to have done the work to learn their trade, however, we do tend to seek the faddish solution in regard to the most important parts of life: marriage, faith, worship, discipline, child-rearing, healing, and happiness. What is it that makes a believer a better follower of Christ? One book? One workshop? One good sermon? A Jesus frisbee? Our culture pushes back at every chance: "Try this and it will work better! It is more efficient!" A visiting missionary was describing his hectic international travel schedule to a local supporting church. One member suggested it would use less money and be more efficient if he did not visit all the supporting churches. "Yes," he said, "but then we would not have this," and he pointed to all the congregants gathered, the rich fellowship, the support, and encouragement. It was a good reminder that as followers of Christ, we are not called to be merely efficient, but rather to be disciples.

Fads also do not encourage long-term reflection, and this may be a reason for why, particularly in evangelical circles, we find "Easy Believism"—that efficiency-directed form of Christianity which offers the gift of "fire insurance" and then a life of pretty much doing whatever we desire after that. That sure is an easy way to live as a Christian, but easy does not mean better. Do not fads often act as an escape from spiritual work? Can a person be a Christian, a disciple of Christ, without remembering discipline? Or what about charity, meditation, focus, prayer, doing, loving? Fads, the New Thing, can push in all the wrong ways; they push us to think about the next thing rather than, say, our next opportunity to sacrifice what we desire for what God desires. The fad can make us think that we control the changes we need to be making, that we can just purchase the solution—when we are ready to do so.

When Fads Entrench

There is another way in which fads influence how we understand them: complacency followed by ignorance. Worry about the pennies and dimes and the dollars will take care of itself, but humans don't do this typically. We often consider the small things small and meaningless and ignore them until later. Consider how one manifestation of fads is that they have been relentless, at least for the past hundred years, in pushing boundaries. (The history of why we follow fads is covered in chapter 4.) The arts fueled this thinking in many ways, as did a kind of squishy Darwinist thinking that pushed the concept of the *avant guard* and the cult of originality. What is easily forgotten in this relentless push ahead are issues of ethics and quality. The newest fad could often be defined as, particularly after the 50s, as the most provocative "next thing." These steps, often very small, seemingly unimportant at the moment, are not tracked by many. Assumptions are made about the latest being best and then twenty or thirty years later, we look up and ask, "What happened?"

It ought not take much reflection to see that within the secular culture that goal of keeping up with the latest has often been one of provocation through descending steps down into sensuality, eroticism, and narcissism. Does the change from the formal, classical music of the eighteenth century to the frivolity of popular music in the nineteenth, to jazz, to Elvis, to rock and roll, to, well, Lady Gaga, represent a qualitative advance?

Sometimes there are practices, thinking, concepts, that start as fads, as a way to be more [*fill in your own word here: timely, efficient, contemporary, relevant, contemprevant, etc.*] and then they kind of hang around, get stuck, become tradition. It is not wrong to suggest that this is what many evangelicals fear about ritual and tradition: it is seen as a way to bypass the really important practices and is little more than a ruse, a dodge, some superficial means of thinking ourselves spiritual. Ritual is thought inauthentic. But all churches practice ritual, of one form or another. Where did they come from? What do they mean?

Here is a good example of slipping, of not watching the details and then winding up where a practicing Christian might not wish to go: most denominations used to have gatherings every Sunday morning, Sunday night, and Wednesday evening. That was fairly typical. Then Sunday nights fell away, then Wednesday night prayer meetings, and now, safe to say, Sunday services are pretty much it for many congregations. We are not directed specifically how and when to meet to worship together, of course, but the point is: How did the decision to cut Sunday and Wednesday evenings come about? Was it to create more opportunity for the brothers and sisters to develop and grow as disciples, to show love to each other? Does anyone even remember this being something discussed and debated, held to Scripture, prayed about?

For a more dramatic example, consider where the secular culture has moved since WWII. It ought not take too much imagination to see the decline. Living together? Easy credit? Sex and violence on television? Prescription drugs? These few examples are pointed out as they grew incrementally, and perhaps from good motives, but what followed? An example with damming effects is no-fault divorce laws. When divorce laws were changed, there were frequently meaningful issues at work: abused wives and children, terrible situations, financial disasters. Now divorce requires very little money and perhaps even less reflection, and we have divorce rates that reflect that. It may seem strange to consider divorce law changes a fad, and yet, this example rather gets to a core problem with fads: the lack of reflection of consequences, of considering that maybe the easy road is not always the best road. Like other entrenched fads, this one is here to stay.

Churches are stuck with their own entrenched fads and find them difficult to dismantle for similar reasons. Firstly, the structures of churches. Many Christian denominations, and of course Catholics, have leadership structures, some with quite elaborate hierarchies. Did these, do these, have unexpected difficulties? Of course, evangelicals thought the hierarchies problematic a long while back and moved to have independent church bodies, but so that our evangelical brothers and sisters are not let off the hook: Do not those who seek to become preachers in evangelical churches attend seminaries with particular hierarchies? And most churches in the developed world do not think twice about hiring a minister, paying him a salary, benefits, vacation time, etc. That is, what was once looked upon (in a significantly different way) as a ministry is now a career, and those employed in that career answer to a hierarchy of one sort or another. It ought to give us pause to consider what it means when a church body can fire their pastor. And it is not merely church leadership that has embraced the business model. Have you ever been "church shopping"? What a perverse idea! We "shop" for a church. Surely that comes from a consumerist mentality that seeks the best value, the best entertainment, the nicest people with the most attractive children, and music that tickles our ears. We are set up, and have been for a long time, to be consumers of church. And it is very, deeply, and terrifyingly entrenched.

What, then, happens when the reasons for a change are lost? Every church does some kind of activity that was started with, at least, rudimentary thinking. Do we even know what those thoughts were, and why we still participate in whatever activity we do? Why are church buildings shaped as they are? Why do we sing in church? Why did pastors/choirs wear robes? Why did some churches scrap the robes? Hard on the heels of forgetting the reasons for why changes were made is the weak thinking that drives making more changes! We start to actually think that we can take actions, make changes, and adopt new styles, and that those "don't mean anything." So, we might hear, for example, when a complaint is made changes in church music, "Don't worry. It's just music, it doesn't mean anything. It's not sinful." And this brings us to plain old stupidity.

Stupidity, Stupid Thinking, and Stupid Actions

There is no doubt that one of the problems of fads is their ability to both fortify and amplify our stupidity. That is to say, we do them because of dumb decisions, and they frequently work to make us even dumber. Something we think a dumb fad: WWJD wristbands. Let's be honest, these were dumb. Sure, wear whatever you like, but don't think that this was aiding in spreading the gospel or making better disciples. In fact, it does not require a stretch to see the wearing of dumb wristbands as an attempt to lower our engagement with others: "I don't have to build relationships, work hard at loving others, remember to follow Christ always—I'm wearing a wristband! Unbelievers can see it and know that I'm a Christian and then ask me questions!" Yeah . . .

But it is worse than that. Why do we find a need to change so much? What motivates that? Does the gospel change? Does Christ change? Does God change? So why do things at church change? One answer is something like, "We've got to be relevant to the culture," and then perhaps offer a strange misinterpretation of what Paul said in Athens. For example, one author opens his book, *God in the Gallery*, by suggesting that Paul's comments on Mars Hill "baptized" pagan poetry, "thus . . . enabling the Spirit to work through those very words."[12] Uh, what? He goes on to build on this idea, suggesting that modern art struggles with "spiritual elements," elements that are on display for the insightful viewer.[13]

When we start following the fad, it leads to more and more fad following. Perhaps it speeds up the adoption of fads in the culture at large, and leads to a lack of patience, of reflection, and an abundance of stupidity. These problems are part of a broader trend of thinking things must *constantly* change. Christians are not called to be stupid. There is a vicious cycle: fads can generate fads and make us unreflective and impulsive and more likely to

12. Seidell, *God in the Gallery*, 11.

13. Part of the mistake Seidell makes can be seen when he writes, "In order for the contemporary church to speak to culture, it is important to have a fuller and more nuanced historical, critical, theoretical, and aesthetic narrative of the development of modern art." Seidell, *God in the Gallery*, 12. Thus his book seeks to find the slightest hint of anything spiritual in artists of the past hundred years. We applaud Seidell for seeking to understand the culture, for trying to understand contemporary art, but we find his opening analysis about Paul at Mars Hill deeply flawed (and really strange), and think that leads to intellectually vapid and ethically destructive valuations of art.

adopt other fads. We are called to be as wise as serpents and as gentle as doves. We are going to make enough mistakes in our lives without being total idiots, so let's try hard not to be idiotic when it comes to church decisions.

Two Examples of Stupidity

As far as we know, there has only been one cinematic effort that took on the task of admonishing Christians for their ill-conceived embrace of stupidity: *The Gospel Blimp* (1967). This film, made and financed by Christians in the late 60s is legendary now not for its cinematic efforts (and clearly not for the effects, nor the sets, nor acting . . .) but for pointing out what is obvious to the humble: sometimes Christians do awfully stupid things when trying to do good. In this case the stupid thing is the purchase, by the congregation, of a blimp, in order to distribute tracts and reach the city for Christ. It ends in disaster, of course, but also with a terrific bit of wisdom: one couple in the church who has been trying to reach their neighbors with the blimp has dinner with them at the end. The neighbors now go to church and they gently admonish the couple; they just wanted friends, wanted some connection, and did not need what the blimp was doing.

The second example is biblical and requires little to be said: Joseph. When he was a young man, Joseph was an idiot, a spoiled, rich idiot. Go back and read Genesis 37 again. It is breathtaking how daft he was. In many ways, he got exactly what he deserved from his brothers. He was stupid and he paid for that. What is beautiful is that God, in his mercy, was able to take Joseph's situation and bring good from it. No doubt God had a plan; no doubt we can do dumb things. God can use us no matter what, and that is good, and a relief most of all because when we start to think we are not stupid, that surely means we still don't get it. So, stupid is bad; worse is not realizing that we are all stupid. We need to do our best, seek to understand and learn, and get back to God's good work.

How frequently is foolishness mentioned in Scripture? The answer to that is: lots.

That is why we need to be open to listen to others, when others say to us: "Hey, know what? That is just stupid." (Of course, we expect them to say that in good old Christian love.) But there is a problem in this regard, a form of thinking that has leeched into the culture at large and often affects Christian thinking, too. It is a bit of postmodern refuse that suggests, poorly, that somehow no one can really be wrong, no one is really dumb, we are all just finding our way—and that everyone's thinking is as good as anyone else's. And of course, that everyone is special. Our culture is currently in the throes of just such a worldview. And yes, it is dumb.

The Postmodern Will and Swisstianity

> The teacher investigated the nature of things and communicated his findings as immutable truths, not because he believed in authority, but because he believed in the immutable nature of things underneath the passing phenomena. In contrast, the visionary [prophet] stands at a given point of the historical (or evolutionary) process, claiming decisive insights: into the meaning of history up until his own time; into the mechanism of future historical process; and into the overall objective mankind has been pursuing, an increasingly clear objective with the terminal situation of utopia. By definition, the visionary considers his own historical moment as privileged, as a point at which things past, present, and future become finally *visible*, ripe for his own all-comprehensive grasp. Man's destiny appears to him as meaningful for the first time—an insight he must communicate to all, for otherwise the moment may be irretrievably lost and history may take a wrong direction.[14]

In the above quote, Molnar contrasts some of the differences between the old and the new, between the "teacher" and the "prophet." These same distinctions, which he made in 1968, are still very much with us. However, the "prophet" with "insight" that seemed

14. Molnar, *Sartre*, 3.

so radical to those who thought the seeking of immutable truths unshakeable is today commonplace and even winning.[15] And it has affected every corner of the culture, including the church.

There is a particular manner in which this corrosive perspective has corrupted Christian thinking. The thinking works like this: Someone who is skeptical of immutable truths puts an idea into the public realm and then steps back and claims the attempt to examine and criticize that idea is out of line. Ideas are intimately connected to the individual, so there can be no separation as there are no truths outside of ourselves to be sought. (Remember, immutable truths are thought untrue.) There grows skepticism regarding any answers to be sought outside of our own desires, or more accurately, our own will. When this way of looking at reality is applied to Christianity, we find things like this:

> Both [Christians and non-Christians] have faith; both require belief. The difference is in the nature and kind of belief. [Graham] Ward argues for a new "politics of believing" as a means to develop a "softer Christian ontology." Rather than talk about what is more truthful, talk about what is more believable, what is more compelling for belief.[16]

We are to no longer seek to understand what is true, but to seek that which is compelling. But who can discern what is compelling to another? What used to be considered reasonable is that what is true is perennially valuable to all thoughtful humans. How might that affect how we study the Bible? Previously, many Christians thought exegesis a good method, that is, the attempt to draw out of a text what it actually means. Now it appears a growing number of Christians are rejecting exegesis for its antithesis, eisegesis. Writes one thoughtful pastor, "Many leaders today either don't have the

15. This is the postmodern moment, a worldview that posits a position that all positions are merely opinion and with absolute conviction, and a straight face, claims that all moral positions are merely constructed by humans. More on postmodernism's corrosive effect is covered in chapter 4.

16. Siedell, *God in the Gallery*, 48. Graham Ward is an Anglican priest and the Regius Professor of Divinity at the University of Oxford.

spiritual gift of teaching or haven't received adequate training, and the unfortunate result is that most of our Bible studies are rife with phrases like, 'What does this text mean to you?' as opposed to, 'What does this text *mean*?'"[17] And thus again denigrated is actual meaning, actual truth, actual wisdom for something rather more to the effect of: "I like this!" Of course, one thing no one likes is being unliked by others, and it all works very conveniently that way. So, what is the problem?

Swisstianity is an attempt to make of Christianity a worldview without offense. Those who promote it desire to remain neutral, a presumption that asserts the position that none can have enough knowledge to confidently assert any position, idea, concept, theology, or value as true—except for the knowledge that can strongly assert the presumption of Swisstianity as true. This issue in the church is also something of a climactic moment in the history of the fad. That is to say, it has elements of entertainment, pride, exclusivity, Gnosticism, and stupidity, all wrapped up in a neat little utterly confusing package. This might be the most destructive fad ever in the history of Christian fads for it expresses, unequivocally, the ultimate problem of the fad: the desire to change the faith to fit our own thinking and desires, in this case, whatever we desire.

Consummerist Christianity

Fueling the fad from bracelets to tragic revisionist theology is a mentality that is hard to avoid. For American Christians, there seems little doubt that a self-centered consumerist mentality drives much of our lives including what we do at church and our faddish thinking. And like some of the other fads mentioned above, it runs in both directions: we are consumers so we seek to find Christian answers that we *like*; soon we start to think that consumerism is how we are to be Christian, to act out our faith is to seek the fad. God is not a fad. God is the opposite of the transitory, the ephemeral, the temporal. Fads are about entertainment,

17. Wilson, *Prodigal Church*, 76.

they are superficial, transitory. They often turn not only stupid but destructive and sinful. In a significant way, all sin is a fad. Think about what sin attempts to offer humans: "This way is better! This way is faster, quicker, more pleasurable, more easily attained!" Sin is *my* way to work out *my* salvation, with *my* choices and preferences. We sin for pretty much the same reasons we follow fads, all of which sounds a whole lot like advertising. We want what we want and, in a consumerist society, we do what we can to get it. But that is not Christianity. Read *The Divine Conspiracy*, and in it you will find the author, Dallas Willard, quickly pointing to a problem:

> It is the failure to understand Jesus and his words as reality and vital information about life that explains why, today, we do not routinely teach those who profess allegiance to him how to do what he said was best. We lead them to profess allegiance to him, or expect them to, and leave them there, devoting our remaining efforts to "attracting" them to this or that.[18]

Something is tragically wrong in many parts of our thinking about the faith. Why have we gone off the rails?

18 Willard, *Divine Conspiracy*, 2.

Our repose is to rejoice in the infinite happiness of God and, on a lower scale, in our own crosses and to desire still more of them, for in them we have the privilege of imitating him and proving our love, and there is nothing dearer to the heart that loves. We shall never lack either this happiness, nor God, nor the Cross.

—CHARLES DE FOUCAULD

4

Why We Do the Fad

The evolutionary principle . . . also produced something far more questionable: the presupposition of progress—that is, the assumption that . . . history was a tale of progressive improvement, so that later forms of society, codes of morality, forms of thought and belief were automatically "higher," more "enlightened," "loftier," than earlier ones.[1]

—BASIL WILLEY

For the cultural power of consumerism, arranged against people who want to hang on to the same old thing, reality is like an iceberg: massive, and much of it beneath the surface so that we don't even notice it's there.[2]

—PHILLIP CAREY

IF YOU HAVE READ this far, and you get why the press for the fad is a significant problem for the church (and most of life), then perhaps

---

1. Willey, *Christianity Past and Present*, 110.
2. Carey, *Good News for Anxious Christians*, 117.

you are starting to wonder just how we ended up where we are. In an important manner of speaking, the Christian is not the slightest bit interested in the fad. We seek the eternal, the lasting, the perennial. We follow and believe because Christ is a rock, *the* Rock. We recognize the current as ephemeral, passing, mundane. It is in the church where temporal divisions, whether racial or socioeconomic, gendered or generational, are overcome, as we are all equally loved and equally sinful before God. If we are seeking the eternal in our faith, and in our understanding of the faith, why do we seek the temporal in so many other aspects of the Christian life? How did we get to this place?

As discussed earlier, it can be a problem when a fad goes on for so long that no one knows its origins and it seems to have had its entire meaning changed. Take for example the Christmas tree. There isn't a lot of documentation for the history of Christmas trees, but we know that the Romans used them, in some manner, as fertility symbols. It appears Christians in Germany started to decorate pine trees in the sixteenth century. Of course, the tree really took off in Victorian England. Would we call this a fad today? Ought we to reject it for its pagan roots? For its Victorian roots? For the fact that most everyone has a Christmas tree even though they don't worship Christ? Should Christians reject having Christmas trees because of the history? How about this as a starting point: might it be a better act of discernment, and discussion, if people were educated about where the traditions of the Christmas tree originated? Being aware of the history and varieties of meaning can help, and not just with holiday traditions, but with some of the origins of how the West became a fad culture.

History of the West

The story of the foundations of Western Civilization is typically thought to begin in ancient Greece. The Greeks were the first to develop some values and concepts which we still hold dear today. For example, the discipline of history prior to Thucydides was based on hearsay; he desired to learn what actually happened and sought a method to do so. Many realms of learning were cultivated by the Greeks: mathematics, a kind of science, poetry, architecture, theatre, physics, astronomy, politics with, of course, democracy. Plato even began to apply reason to the study of theology, something previously unheard of. It is critical to remember, however, that what lay behind most of these studies, these attempts to gain knowledge, was the desire to know what was true, and the Greeks meant this in a broad sense: not just what was accurate to reality, to our senses, but meaningful to understand. They attempted to grasp truth for all aspects of human existence.

This is an important step in human learning that is essential to comprehend, but one that, as a result of later changes in thinking, has been rather shoved into the dustbin of history. The Greeks wanted to find answers—truth—in all realms of learning. They did not wish to merely find out how to make the most efficient temple, or grow grapes with greater volume. They wanted to know why humans are here, what the best way for humans to live in groups might be, and why anyone should struggle to be ethically good; indeed, they even asked what was meant by ethically "good." Using reason in ways that it had not been used before, they made tremendous strides in seeking genuine knowledge, not merely opinion.

The Romans appreciated the skill the Greek mind brought to things, but they were more interested in efficiency, in how to politically manage a vast empire with diverse peoples; they were not after what the Greeks sought. It wasn't until the medieval age that human intellects began again to be directed towards perennial questions, but this time, of course, aided by knowledge of God and Scripture. Medieval philosophers, who were typically priests, read the Greeks, read the Romans, and read their Bibles. They used their minds, aided by reason, informed by tradition and Scripture, and guided by faith, to struggle with questions. Like the Greeks, they too thought there existed genuine knowledge, real answers, truth, and it was a human duty to use the mental equipment God provided to seek them. And then came the Renaissance.

Attempting to make historical epochs more than they actually were works well for the dramatization of history, but it is less satisfactory for knowing what really went on; it is easy to overstate and to understate. Clearly, Western thinking changed as a result of what started in Italy in the fourteenth century, and one of those changes, for good and ill, was the rise of science.[3] Galileo's exploits discovered a better way to do science, but a less good way to do philosophy. We think a good shorthand comment on this critical change is offered by C.S. Lewis:

> The real reason why Copernicus raised no ripple and Galileo raised a storm, may well be that whereas the one offered a new supposal about celestial motions, the other insisted on treating this supposal as fact. If so, the real revolution consisted not in a new theory of the heavens but in a "new theory of the nature of theory."[4]

The idea of a theory of celestial motions being posited as fact was a change in thinking that also changed thinking. Galileo, and what would become empirical science, that is, science based on observation and the senses, was new. Soon after, Francis Bacon came up with a system, the Scientific Method, that we all learned in school. What sprang from all this was quite astonishing, opening up the physical world for the benefit of humans. Unfortunately, human vanity being what it is, not only was any connection to the medieval notion of "natural philosophy" (the enriching pursuit of knowledge of the physical world as a reflection of the Divine Mind) gone, but soon empiricism was directed, during the so-called Enlightenment, towards the non-physical in the hopes of unlocking it, as had been accomplished in the material realm. When empiricism attempts to discern knowledge beyond its kin, however, practicality and efficiency often take the place of wisdom and virtue.

What might humans have learned from the unfolding events of the Renaissance, the Reformation, and the Enlightenment? Surely not the least thing learned is that human minds can crack open

---

3. For an in-depth look at how the embrace of science affected culture, see Pontyen and Miller, *Western Culture at the American Crossroads*.

4. Lewis, *Discarded Image*, 16. For a more extensive and effective discussion of Lewis's take on this moment, see Root, *C.S. Lewis and a Problem of Evil*.

the physical realm to, sometimes, good effect, that humans can seek to emulate a previous culture and remake their own, that the most significant social institution, the church, could both be deeply flawed but also rejected and remade, and that even fundamental political structures could be undone. That is to say, a notion of progress, improvement, and change was embedded into thinking.

And then the horse was loosed, the cat was out of the bag, and Pandora's box was opened in the nineteenth century. Those clever rules of science that unlocked so much were now directed towards many other realms of knowledge. Consider what Marx did for history and politics: What drives men, fuels their motives, determines history? Economics! Sure, everyone used to think it had to do with pleasing God, following eternal principles handed down through centuries, but no, they were all wrong. And this march, or race, or stampede, continued through the century. Freud determined everyone had been wrong about human behavior and motivation. Rousseau stated that it would have been better for all to remain in a "natural" state and everyone was wrong about the benefits of being civilized and cultured. Manet painted what he saw in front of him: drunkards, prostitutes, and terrible working conditions; everyone who painted an ideal previously was wrong. This relentless push for "progress" reached a climactic moment with, of course, Darwin's Theory of Evolution that no doubt was responding to what seemed, by this point, to be a normal course of events (we are all wrong and have to change), but also encouraged more change. Very quickly, the notion of evolving stuck and writers like Herbert Spencer developed the lovely idea of Social Darwinism. Our point in all of this: by the time Darwin published his book, the pump was primed for the belief that all must constantly be changing or, if you like, evolving. Add the benefits of science, the goodness that came with some democracies, and the seemingly endless improvements in technology, and it is not hard to see why Western Civilization jumped on the bandwagon of "progress." Out of the cauldron of progress have come many elements. We point out five of them that direct and fuel a culture of fad.

Evolving Culture

Once the notion of evolution stuck in regard to the material realm, quickly came the notion that human culture, too, is changing. It did not take much education to know that humans had lived differently prior to the American and French Revolutions, nor did it take much insight to grasp that there were advantages to the freedoms available in a democracy. Life had improved. With a heavy dose of poetic liberty, we could quickly attempt to invoke the concept of evolution to suppose that culture, the context for human life, was improving. The simple formula was established: improving meant change and change meant improvement.

The change came rapidly. As is frequently the case, it became most publically manifest in the arts (as discussed below), but change developed in every area of human thought and activity. One example is education. Previously, students were require to study classical languages and writers. The goal had to do with character development and understanding rather than job skills. Thomas Jefferson decided this would not suit the new country of the United State, and at the University of Virginia he offered instead courses in science and agriculture.[5] John Dewey formalized this approach, changing education profoundly. His thinking is symptomatic of the problem. Writes Molnar:

> This conviction is at the root of John Dewey's education theories, which he elaborated in the name of what he considered a radically changing world, waiting to be "reconstructed." His successors have made the *concept of change* and the *preparation for change* veritable articles of faith. Henceforward, no philosophy may be credited with enough truth-value to warrant its adoption as common system of references. Philosophies, at least the traditional kinds, are labeled "static," meaning that they are upheld only by the mentally unadjusted or those who remain loyal for selfish or sinister reasons to such institutions

---

5. Notably, Jefferson made no provision for a chapel at the university.

and cultural values whose very survival in a progressive age is considered anachronistic and retrogressive.[6]

And who wants to be anachronistic and retrogressive? We do not need to hang onto the past—that is where all the problems started. We need change! We need the new! The times they are a-changing! Culture is moving ahead, we are advancing! Of course, as with evolutionary biology, we may well ask: Advancing towards what? What criteria is, or ought to be, used to determine what constitutes an advance?[7]

Democracy, Individualism, and Consumerism

One answer to the question of qualitative advance has been: "Whatever I wish to define as an advance." Consider some distinctions between the individual in a democracy and the individual in a monarchy. Clearly, there are legal differences, such as what we can and cannot do, freedom of speech, and due process, to name a few. Under an absolute monarch, we did what we were told. Period. We would not be brought before a king and be told, "Go and do this job," and then reply, "Yes, but first, I have a few thoughts on why I should do another job." This did not happen. But in a democracy, well, that's a different story. Not only can we choose whatever type of work we wish, and quit it anytime, but we can, almost without limits (at least in America), say whatever we like in whatever context where we might wish to say it.

6. Molnar, *Future of Education*, 70. Molnar continues a few pages later: "It is often claimed today in the name of 'science' and 'scientific objectivity' that education should remain neutral in regard to philosophic and moral issues. But if such a condition is permitted to exist, then the young men and women who do not live in a vacuum will not *elaborate* their own philosophy of life but *absorb* a crude and simplified concoction derived from the prevailing mood around them. In other words, if the schools (and the parents) do not assume this responsibility, other social forces will." Molnar, *Future of Education*, 86.

7. Just in case the reader has doubts about our point, we would have you consider that despite all the technological and even social advances of the twentieth century, it still managed to be the most bloody in all of human history, by a wide margin.

Independence is held up as a goal, as a virtue; in a way, as an ethic. No one should tell you what to do! Stand on your own two feet, decide for yourself, don't be a "yes" man, show initiative! You are an individual! However, the believer understands individuality in a way profoundly different from those who do not follow Christ. Believers grasp that they are individually responsible before God for their actions, that while they attend church with others, and while they are called to be part of a fellowship, it does not absolve them of their own behavior. We recognize that all individual humans have a value to God. All possess an eternal soul which we ought to direct towards the truth.

It is, of course, just a small step from a humble recognition of our position before God as an individual towards our removing God from that and fueling our individual ego. Who do those other schmucks think they are? I know I am my own man and I get to decide things for myself! Part of the illusion when in the throes of being independent is that our decisions are driven by all sorts of other elements beside our coolly rational minds: genetics, upbringing, social factors. But that is never forgotten by those involved in selling things. Hand-in-hand with American thinking about independence is the relentless push of consumerism.

Fads are by definition transitory and superficial. This does not mean, of course, that they are impotent. Fads can drive all sorts of cultural trends, often not in a good way. One example: kitchen design. Ought it not to strike us as freakishly weird that we care about in what style our kitchens are constructed? Kitchens have a nearly utterly pragmatic function (with some important family aspects, no doubt), and we use them daily in messy and often smelly ways. We need a space to prepare, clean food, cook food, cool food, store food, and wash everything when done. Yet this rather simple need for a functional space is transformed into a faddish desire to keep up with the Joneses. So, we spend thousands on granite, new cupboards, and new stoves with newer, modern, contemporary designs. The thought of an out-of-style kitchen is, well, just plain embarrassing. Is there much that is more trivial than to be ashamed because our kitchen is somehow out of date? And this overwhelming consumerist cultural effect plays on Christians in their culture, and we try and make the faith work in similar ways.

The consumerist mentality, a prime motivator of the fad, is always driving the consumer on to the next thing.[8] We've got to have the next thing to "keep up" or "keep current" and "not get behind." There are plenty of pitches from the culture to keep us looking ahead. This destroys any notion of seeking quiet wisdom, of focusing on what we have. No point in considering carefully and deeply, since what *really* matters is whatever experience, item, idea, book, event, or person is going to be the next thing. Carey posits a new type of guilt, one driven by a consumer culture:

> What makes a good consumer is a short attention span, meaning that you quickly get tired of the same old thing and keep wanting to get new things—lots of new things. People who are content to stay within their comfort zone are not very useful to the many organizations that are intent on expanding their share of the market. So, if you're one of those people who likes to be faithful and hang on to old things—old doctrines, old people in your life—then major cultural forces will be marshaled against you.[9]

It is not difficult to imagine similar thinking occurring in the church. We are neck-deep in this culture and it affects us every day. It's worth asking every day: Is there a significant difference between regarding ourselves as Christian consumers or as disciples of Christ? Perhaps more to the point: ought we be thinking about ourselves at all? If we are disciples, if we seek the "old things," we

8. Consumerist fads affect thinking within the academy, sacred and secular. What do we expect seminaries and universities and colleges to do, exactly? There are perennial truths that are sought, examined, disseminated, but not new truth. However, seminaries are often tainted by exactly the same problem as their secular peers: originality. That is to say, often it is the faddish that gets the most publishing, the most buzz, the greatest rewards and careers. So how does this work in seminaries? Seems a huge conflict of interest: colleges want to have hot-shot professors to raise the stature of their school. Hot-shot professors usually get that way from publishing hot-shot books—books that may, or may not, be terribly valuable. See the problem?

9. Carey, *Good News for Anxious Christians*, 117.

must be conscious of the pernicious effects of consumerism. Besides denigrating and chipping away at the seeking of the perennial, consumerist culture, the culture of the fad, also consistently seeks to avoid quality by becoming about me and my desires.

The Aesthetic Shift

One of the monumental effects of the shifts in Western Civilization discussed earlier was the growing skepticism towards the truth. The shift towards philosophical relativism claims that there is no solid ground; in nearly every human civilization that ever existed, people thought there was real truth, knowledge that was universally true: true for all people in all places at all times. That once broadly accepted way of looking at reality has been hammered at over the past few centuries and has produced some of what was discussed earlier in this chapter.[10] It also has produced an obsession with the aesthetic. The term was first used in the mid-eighteenth century, and it has to do with sensation and emotional response and it makes sense how it fits with philosophical skepticism: If there is no longer an objective to which we may aspire, then what have we left to direct us other than feelings, desires, passions, that is, the aesthetic. My passions tell me this and that and I follow them.

It ought to be clear how this had a profound effect on the fad. If there is one thing we know about feelings, it is that they can be fleeting and superficial, particularly when the goal is to stimulate more feelings, and particularly when humans desire

---

10. In case you are pondering the reasonableness of relativism, here are two arguments for why it is daft. First, who wants to claim that the evil of murder, rape, and slavery are merely opinion? Really, if we discovered a culture somewhere that thought those were good, would we just shrug and say, "Well, live and let live"? We may consider here the issues of female circumcision in some cultures. Ought that be something that, say, sensible and ethical humans ought to work to stop? Second, relativism claims that that no knowledge, typically beyond material knowledge, can be true. Can a relativist use science to demonstrate that relativism is true? More to the point, isn't any relativist forced to claim, with as much faith as any believer, and no science, that their view of the world is true?

entertainment. And if there is no longer truth to be sought, well, then there sure is entertainment to be sought. How that plays out was seen in the art world of the late nineteenth and most of the twentieth centuries.[11] What it has left is a tragic wreck of a culture wherein what is demanded is a steady stream of cultural products that stimulate and entertain but do not improve, for what can now be meant by "improvement"? Driving it forward was the cult of originality, obviously influential in fads (in art and in culture and in the church), and something not terribly compatible with the faith. Can we be original? Or is there nothing new under the sun? What really matters in regard to how we advance? What do we mean by advance, evolve, develop? What does it mean when Christians talk about growth? Same thing? Maybe more to the point: Is seeking originality, or a fad, really what Christ desires?

How did Christians think about this previously? The history of church architecture was based originally on Roman law courts, because it would have been inappropriate to base them on Roman pagan temples, and the shape of the church was early established and its basic function and meaning made sense. It was followed for more than a thousand years. The manner in which icons are still painted in certain corners of Christendom follows precedent laid down more than a millennium ago. And there have been and remain groups of Christians who do not seek to follow the world's values when it comes to trends and fads. Various Mennonite groups to this day do not follow fashion trends in clothing, hairstyles, nor in most other aspects of their lives.

---

11. In brief, Manet sought what he called realism. Courbet, also a realist, claimed he could not paint an angel as he'd never seen one. In short order followed other attempts to capture the "real," whatever was meant by that, which at one time or another seemed everything: Renoir's parties, Monet's optical sensations, Gaugin's objects of his sexual gratification, young Tahitian girls, Degas' bodies (ballerinas) in action, and many more. Modern (as it was called) art culminated in the dreadfully serious and astonishingly vapid movement of abstract expressionism, upon which all the hopes of capturing a pure aesthetic rode. The often vast fields of colors were met with success only in the rarified realms of the "art world." Normal folks, who actually used to enjoy going to art museums, checked out.

Being Christian in a Fad Culture

So why do we do the fad? No doubt there will always be a tension between "living in the world" yet "not being of the world," and we are persuaded that God does call us to be in it, but this world we are in celebrates a culture that is faddish to its core. And this creates a unique problem for Christians of the contemporary world: How to reach this fad culture? On the one hand, we struggle to not get caught up in the trivial. On the other hand, we want to reach the culture where it is at. How does a Christian do that, reach out to those in the culture, if the culture, and its products and systems, are corrupt and corrupting? How can we follow their lead in style (and thus a fad) if it is bad (in a broad sense)? To be in immersed in a culture is a risky and scary thing. It requires wit and courage and prayer and support and being as clever as serpents to negotiate.

Can Christians create television programs that do not sell out the faith? Or is TV intrinsically about little more than entertainment, fluff, and commercialization? Ought Christians take a style of music invented by the world—for example, rock—and put Christian words on it? Or does the style of the music have a meaning of its own that is incompatible with Christian teaching? What does the Christian offer the culture from the inside if the inside of the culture is based on trivialities, aesthetics, entertainment, and often debauchery? Is it possible to work inside this environment? Some Christians, when they attempt to do so, end up following fads sort of through the back door; if the culture is following fads and we need to engage the culture, ought we offer Christian fads in an attempt to attract more to the faith?

In a culture that demonstrates skepticism toward the truth, fosters independence that can be taken to stroke vanity, emphasizes an endless drive towards consumerism, and then promotes cultural products that aim to do little besides please our aesthetic desires, it is no wonder that what is produced are people of the fad. People of the fad have at least the following characteristics:

We Are Bored

Americans get bored. Fads have trickled in from our culture in a steady stream and now we are dependent upon them. We want the new and if we do not get it, tedium. We are bored frequently. Maybe most of the time. One kind of boredom, well-deserved to be called boring, is when the person or event doing the talking or performing is just terribly dull and is so because the product offer was poorly executed. In other words, the Thing is just rubbish. We legitimately get bored at that. The other kind of boredom, however, stems from our being stupid and dull and not actually being sophisticated enough to grasp what is being presented. That is to say, we are quick to dismiss something that might be worth a second look, listen, or read. We may also be too quick to dismiss the Thing and miss out on a charitable look for the goodness in what is being presented. But it is so easy to do what we do with the remote: "I don't like it" and on to the Next Thing.

Wannabe

No one wants to be on the outside, out of the group. We all desire to be fashionable, well thought of, hip, liked, not stuck in the mud. We want attention. We want to be cool. Why else do we do the fad? It is about keeping up with the Joneses, but also keeping ahead of the Joneses, too. Very weird, and a bit scary, to think about why we do this, why we must get the Next Thing. We want to be liked but also admired, but why would anyone want to be admired for the sorts of clothes they wear? Surely, for the Christian (or any rational human), an individual ought to be admired for traits that are admirable, worthy of admiration—not fashion, not being hip. Easy to see how the world, with the destruction of an objective to seek after and struggle to learn, without Christ to follow, needs to find some means of satisfaction and meaning. Or, at least, just a way to get some kind of approval from others.

Lazy

Lingering behind many human efforts is a general desire to be lazy. Now imagine a culture that does not really believe there is much wisdom towards which its mental capacity ought to be directed, a culture that sees the point of its existence is to entertain and keep boredom at bay, and it is not difficult to see how a desire to relax and take it easy is endemic. Our culture seems to grasp discipline as a means to an end, as long at that end is material: athletes should train hard, students should study hard, but all of it ought to pay off in some manner.

The idea of spiritual discipline gets lost in a quiet sort of shuffling off. Do we really need to follow the gospel? It is easier just to pay no attention to any sort of notion of spiritual exercise, daily disciplines of prayer and reading, or daily dying to self. So, along with the culture in general, we too seek an easier path, one that will provide us comfort when we wish it. Perhaps worse than the world is that, while we ought to know better, we come up with a host of excuses: "Discipline? Just another word for works!"; "God knows what I'm capable of doing, he made me!"; "I'm not perfect, just forgiven." We come up with lots of stupid thinking.

Stupid

There is something to be said for our just being stupid and going with the flow. We are raised in a culture that has, for quite some time, appreciated greatly our being daft and thoughtless when it comes to, well, pretty much everything. Politicians don't want anyone to be smart because they might realize they aren't doing the jobs we voted them into office to do; bad teachers do not wish to have thoughtful students, as they are more work; and marketers don't want any conscious thoughts at all because then we might start to realize that all the mindless purchasing and obsessing is stupid. We want to be the smartest, most up-to-date, hippest, most thoughtful. Notably, we don't want to be the ones who suffer the most, who give the most away, who struggle the most. We know, deep down, one solid path to good health: diet and exercise. Yet how many millions are spent each year on diet pills, diet programs, diet drinks, and foods? Somehow, we imagine we will find success without the discipline of diet and exercise.

Christians know that we need to study and pray but, waaa, that is tough. Thus, if we can find the magic solution (think Prayer of Jabez, or praying the hours), it will be less work than the real business of prayer and study and thinking and loving. Yet we continue with fads, we continue with them even when we know they are stupid. Certainly, all of us are constantly and habitually susceptible to sin, but it also appears we are equally susceptible to stupidity. That may be, in large part, because we just have not taken the time to learn, to read, to think; we just do not realize there are genuinely better alternatives out there. Discernment is something to be worked at, struggled for, but only for those who are seeking more than a lazy faith.

Scared

We are scared. If you do not think you are scared, consider the excuses you came up with the last time you were in a situation during which you should have shared your faith, spoken up, stepped out in faith, loved the unlovely. The excuses come fast: we are scared of being uncool, not being relevant, looking dumb, offending, appearing patronizing, or just plain being embarrassed.

We attempt various methods of accommodation, but we cannot argue, or dance, paint, reason, spend, entertain, print, sing, or perform our way out of the duty to love our neighbors. Has the church grown weary of being on the outside, not being part of the inner circle? It seems so. And when those fears develop, we frequently follow the fads, those that attempt to accommodate. Of course, we know accommodating, feeling comfortable is not the right path. Francis Schaeffer noted several ways Christian have compromised: distortion of Scripture, confusing God's Kingdom with socialistic programs, extreme feminism, easy divorce, homosexuality, and abortion. Said Schaeffer, "When evangelicals accommodate themselves to this kind of thinking, which began with the Enlightenment, they end up bending Scripture to meet the changing, flowing winds of our culture rather than judging culture by the absolutes of Scripture."[12] Scripture guides us with such as these from Paul: "Am I now trying to win the approval of human beings, or of God? Or am I trying to please people? If I were still trying to please people, I would not be a servant of Christ" (Gal. 1:10).

During a lecture question and answer by Dr. Michael Ramsden, one of the attendees asks about reported news stories:

> A lady, Christian, social worker, who was very well thought of, did a wonderful job, had the temerity to suggest that marriage was best between a man and a woman and that children were better off with a mother and father. And for saying that she lost her job. A pastor in Northern Ireland was preaching, the thing was being live-streamed, and he said something similar, and somebody complained, and he was taken to court. I'm just wondering what's the balance between wise as serpents and harmless as doves but yet standing for truth.

Ramsden replied:

> I'm not aware of any effective model for discipleship in the church of Jesus Christ that doesn't cost everything. I think what's happened in the West is that we've partly developed models of discipleship that don't demand everything, cost very little, and don't produce anything.[13]

Ego

Think of how all the elements of the fad culture work towards this end. There is no other end towards which we might aim, it is thought by some, for what is meant by "end," other than what we

12. Quoted in Delahoyde, "Are Christians Headed for Disaster?," 19. Think the church is accommodating more, or less, since 1984?

13. Ramsden, "Michael Ramsden Q&A."

desire and prefer? And one thing all humans desire is to feel pretty good about themselves and what they desire and prefer. Human pride is a constant temptation, a constant threat. It is so easy to believe that some *thing*, whatever it is, makes us better, smarter, and ahead of the curve. That strokes our egos, our constantly needy egos. We learn of a fad, particularly before everyone else, and it just gives us that extra bit of better-than-you. And then we learn it is just a fad, so we drop it, before everyone else, and that gives us just a little bit more. It is how the culture currently works and, as we have seen, there is much to tempt and trip-up the believer.

Swisstianity:
An Example of the Culture Directing the Faith

In this chapter, we have been seeking reasons for why Christians pursue the fad. The answer we have proposed is: because we are caught up in the secular culture. A grand example of this, as discussed previously, is the current fad of Swisstianity. This fad has all the elements and sits squarely in the secular culture's fad of the moment. We do not think it any sort of accident that at the same time our culture is moving away from thinking reality has answers and towards postmodern skepticism, some Christians find the latter more appealing. Those who embrace some version of Swisstianty typically reject exegesis for eisegesis, reject tradition, are scared of being on the cultural outs, seek aesthetic experience, promote a sort of consumerism, and are, at the end of the day, practicing something stupid. Swisstianity. Yep, it has a bit of everything.

Does the faith evolve? Or do we grow? When we think of Christianity as evolving, it means things will change. But which things and how much and when do we lose sight of fundamentals? And are there fundamentals anymore? But oh, how tempted we all are to make those small "comfort" changes. You know, those changes "for the better." Small errors are hard to challenge when they are small. The problems manifest later down the road after they add up. The problem of this ultimate Christian fad is in thinking we can remake, again and again, the faith into anything we like.

When the culture seeks the satisfaction of its aesthetic preferences, it has a rather sideways effect of reducing all to aesthetic
preferences. Christians should know better, but Swisstians have a
nifty out for this: If some claim there are problems with the New
Thing, the Swisstians merely reply, "Yes, but that is just an expression of your preferences." It is all about preferences unless it is
mine against yours and then mine are better.

Fear of being irrelevant to the culture, or thinking themselves
unable to communicate with non-Christians, or uncool, somehow
threw a switch for various Christians who thought Swisstianity
a new, and better, way to follow Christ. This new fad manifests
itself in all sorts of new books, controversial speakers and hipster
videos (see the Emergent Church, or Rob Bell, but they aren't the
only ones). It seduced and continues to seduce many and brought
skepticism to the faith. Did it increase the numbers of believers,
disciples, those giving their lives to Christ? Did anyone keep score?

Swisstianity is just not a bright way to make the faith attractive to the world nor an intelligent way to think. For the reader
wondering just why this way of thinking is so utterly daft, we offer
the following brief rebuttal: (1) Human beings cannot *not* have a
position, a philosophy, a worldview. (2) To say that we cannot have
firm answers about a particular issue is to offer a firm answer. Or to
put this another way: to make the claim "There are no true answers"
is to offer an answer to the issue of answers, and one that is held to
be true. (3) Either the Bible has some answers or it does not. If we
cannot stand convinced of the truth of Christ's divine nature, his
death, resurrection, and the grace offered, well, then we have nothing. The better way of dealing with our own limited pea-brains, as
suggested by Paul, is to consider that we see but through a glass
darkly. Of course, we have confidence in the truth of the Scriptures;
we ought also have humility that we do not know all. We aspire to
learn and to grow. And this is exactly what Swisstianity, and indeed
the postmodern worldview, prevents us from doing, for what could
possibly be outside of our own self that is worth knowing?

Fads currently urge us to stop thinking and to just depend
upon the Next Thing. There is something critical and essential to

ideas for the believer. Part of our faith is grounded in a book. That implies reading and learning and thinking. We need to consider the ideas, all of the ideas. For example, love your neighbor as yourself. Yeah, how? How is that accomplished? We need to carefully consider. But what role do ideas play in our faith? Some, when they either tire or do not understand theological reading, when they weary of plowing through Calvin or McLaren or Carson, take a retreat position and say, "Who needs these kinds of books, anyway? We're just to love Jesus and follow him!" It should go without saying that while that is true, that also trivializes the Christian life. HOW do we love Jesus and HOW do we follow him? And a host of other questions follow. What Christians need to consider, in regard to ideas, is their value. Which is more important, the ideas we hold or the actions we take? It must be and remain the former, our ideas, as it is these that direct our actions. Will our actions take us to good ideas? And what are we talking about when we say "good ideas"?

This cuts both ways in that we need to actually think about our ideas and be careful about what we embrace and what we reject. Ideas matter as they are what inform our behavior. We are what we think. We do indeed need to ask, "Why do we do that?" or "Why do we do it that way?" However, if we ask "why," but don't bother to seek out the answer, we may end up reinventing the wheel, or worse.

5

The Faddish and the Enduring,
a Qualitative Difference

[M]etrics can record the frequency of our church attendance,
the regularity of our Bible reading and the exact amount of our
tithing, but they can never gauge the genuineness of any of them,
or whether they are any better than "the noise of the solemn
assemblies" against which the prophets fulminated.[1]

—OS GUINNESS

The Innovator

AMERICANS LIKE PARTICULAR KINDS of stories, stories that are
both examples of the American Dream and stories that are exem-
plars for how we might wish that dream to progress. A particular
story is the Innovator Story. Its progenitor is the rags-to-riches
story of the virtuous young man who struggles magnificently and
through tremendous odds. At the end of the story, this exemplar
has produced something new, better, improved, more rational,
more human, and at a lower cost. We like better. We like improved.

1. Guinness, *Renaissance*, 43.

Who doesn't? But the Innovator Story often comes with a twist. Frequently, it contains something of The Underdog Story (and perhaps so with or without the Innovator's consent). The Story often becomes less about the virtues of innovation and more about sticking it to the man.

We may consider the story of Elon Musk. His story gets described as an "American Story." He blazed his own trail; he is an original. Musk was not a car engineer but he had a simple question: Could cell-phone batteries provide enough energy for a car? They seem to be pretty amazing as batteries go. Because he was wealthy, he could afford to spend money to follow that vision. And he did. The rest of the story is the stuff of American Dreams. He went against giant auto manufacturers and threw it down when they said "Impossible!" He started a company when it seemed ridiculously problematic. Even the automotive journalists thought it nuts. And then he succeeded. And we love those kinds of stories. American brilliance, hard work, sticking it to the Big Guy when you are the underdog. Yes, that's it! That's how it ought to work! The greatness of human ingenuity and determination! Innovation at its finest.

In many ways, that story is a kind of model for how many see history unfolding. Paradigm shifts, to use a well-worn phrase, are expected. Most of these stories, as you can imagine, spring up during the modern period as science grew in prestige.[2] Any number of examples abound, but Galileo is the classic story: he understood, he was the underdog who fought off the older, entrenched, dogmatic authorities and brought us all into a brilliant new understanding of the movement of the heavenly bodies. And that is how we like it, how we think of history unfolding, of each new generation taking its place, advancing humanity, culturally evolving. That is to say, we extrapolate from scientific and technical accomplishment other sorts of advancement.

2. Ironically, science has become an authority of its own and still manages to often claim for itself a place that it does not deserve. See Pontynen and Miller, *Western Culture at the American Crossroads*.

One effect of drawing conclusions about non-scientific advancement (in the same way we may see scientific progress) is that it produces the profoundly wrong idea that right now, the current moment, is the best. Sure, grandmother and grandfather were lovely people, very kind and sweet, but they didn't quite get it—not like we get it *now*. Oh, the deliciousness of chronocentrism! It all strokes the ego for us because we *get it* and can think we are great and advanced and more thoughtful and better; those with whom we compare ourselves make excellent strawmen especially if they can't fight back because they are long dead. *Now we understand* is often followed by shocking hubris. *Now we can grasp* that human sexuality is to be self-defined. *Now we perceive* that human behavior ought to be guided by our own inner needs. *Now we understand* morality has no basis other than consensual choice.

Perhaps in no clearer way has choronocentrism dominated Western culture over the past two centuries than in regard to morality; specifically, sex. For example, Aldous Huxley wrote:

> For myself as, no doubt, for most of my contemporaries, the philosophy of meaninglessness was essentially an instrument of liberation. The liberation we desired was simultaneously liberation from a certain political and economic system and liberation from a certain system of morality. We objected to the morality because it interfered with our sexual freedom; we objected to the political and economic system because it was unjust. The supporters of these systems claimed that in some way they embodied the meaning (a Christian meaning, they insisted) of the world. There was an admirably simple method of confuting these people and at the same time justifying ourselves in our political and erotic revolt: we could deny that the world had any meaning whatsoever . . . [3]

Now we understand that the world has no meaning (meaning we are free to have as much sex as we can get). But of course, this

3. Huxley, *Ends and Means*, 316. We should point out here that Huxley wrestled with meaning in life and this quote can be read as his criticism of the view that the world is meaningless. Yet we may take him to task for not having a good, meaningful answer.

was a long process. We all, the culture, the West, had to "evolve" to this point. And we all know already the path of that evolution: Not that long ago, showing a married couple in bed together was censored on television because our great-grandparents thought it inappropriate. Now we laugh at that. Sexual behavior was thought by our grandparents to be properly sublimated within a marriage relationship. Now we laugh at that. Non-heterosexual behavior was thought perverse and irrational. We aren't laughing anymore.

In this one example, sexual behavior, we have reaped (and are reaping) what we sowed, because with gloriously self-deceptive hubris we have persuaded ourselves now is the best of times, the most sophisticated of times, the wisest of times. What brave and courageous warriors we have been! With just a bit of reflection, it is clear that not all stories of "brave crusaders" fighting for some kinds of new change have happy endings. But what is the difference, how do we know, when the New Thing is a true and good change or when it is filled with hubris and tragedy?

Discerning the Enduring from the Faddish

We have considered how often little thought is given by American Christians to church changes and that we tend to drift along with the larger culture and bounce from the Newest Thing to the Newestest Thing. As seen in the previous chapters, we tend to embrace that false maxim, "Newer is better. " We suffer from what Screwtape calls the horror of the "Same Old Thing,"[4] and we neglect to present the Rock in a world of shifting sand, all to the detriment of bringing hope and comfort to this world and, many times, to the detriment of the faith itself.

So how ought Christians think about change and the faith? Generally, we think change is good. While the preceding chapters have focused on the negative aspects of the Fad, it is worth pointing out that the other side, progress, can be real and good. We know that change, newness, may refresh, invigorate, redirect, and

---

4 Lewis, *Screwtape Letters*, 50.

encourage. God makes the sun rise every day, and every day that sunrise is not like the one that went before. He made us creative persons. And, of course, we know what it means when the faith becomes encrusted with tradition, ritual, and routine, when we dumbly go through the motions, when following dried up accretions is presumed to be faithfulness. Dead faith is not the goal for Christians. What remains, then, is how to discern between proper growth, advance, creativity, and the trivializations of the Fad.

How does a believer make the distinction between the superficial—the faddish—and the qualitative, that which is accurate, more true, superior, useful, edifying? Are the proponents of the New Thing even considering quality when examining, exploring, predicting, and offering their product? This is difficult to do when we cannot distinguish quality. In order to measure if a change has a genuine qualitative advance, we must have an idea as to what quality means, what quality is. A qualitative change is one that is better, but what does *better* mean?

Where that leaves things is not so simple. Never make changes? Seems less than constructive and more, well, dead. What is it that changes in church? What is it that should change? And why should it change? (Not always the same reasons.) Consider that in the history of Christianity, we have changed from a single centralized church hierarchy to, in some cases, churches entirely on their own. Protestants have dropped some ritual in favor of non-ritual ritual. We had no music, then we had singing, then music was added for singing by congregants, then we published books of those songs, then we started to change the style of music and project the words. We used to care a great deal about smells and bells, gowns and processions but, in some cases, dropped much of that for informal immediacy. Of course, in many ways it is difficult to make generalizations across broad denominational lines, but after Vatican II—when we saw priests and nuns standing by the altar playing guitars and singing—well, probably no Christian groups anywhere were off limits for change. It is worth considering those changes, why they were proposed, and if they had the promised effects.[5]

5. A major contention of this book is that rarely does reflection over

What about some things that do not change, or we do not expect to change, or we aspire to hold on to? Writes the Apostle Peter:

> His divine power has given us everything we need for a godly life through our knowledge of him who called us by his own glory and goodness. Through these he has given us his very great and precious promises, so that through them you may participate in the divine nature, having escaped the corruption in the world caused by evil desires. For this very reason, make every effort to add to your faith goodness; and to goodness, knowledge; and to knowledge, self-control; and to self-control, perseverance; and to perseverance, godliness; and to godliness, mutual affection; and to mutual affection, love. For if you possess these qualities in increasing measure, they will keep you from being ineffective and unproductive in your knowledge of our Lord Jesus Christ. But whoever does not have them is nearsighted and blind, forgetting that they have been cleansed from their past sins. Therefore, my brothers and sisters, make every effort to confirm your calling and election. For if you do these things, you will never stumble, and you will receive a rich welcome into the eternal kingdom of our Lord and Savior Jesus Christ. (2 Pet 1:3–11)

Where is the fad in all that? Faith, goodness, knowledge, self-control, perseverance, godliness, mutual affection, and love, to which we might easily add charity, friendliness, and worship as values in the faith which we do not wish to lose. How much do these change? And yet, *how* we work them out changes. This working out is part of our Christian freedom. The Bible does not write this in stone. We are not given a series of ritualistic practices that will somehow make us all either more devout, more faithful, or make God happy. And we know that significant, shatteringly important

---

changes occur. Much like the rest of the world, Christians run towards the new, grab a hold of some changes that appear flashy, or in response to a real or imagined problem, and don't look back. These changes may be small, no longer having choirs wear robes, or large, questioning the divine nature of Christ; given that numbers in some denominations have been shrinking, it seems some ought to give time to pondering the wisdom of changes already made.

changes, improvements, have been made to practices of the faith, to our understanding of how to work it out.

Work it out. How? With fear and trembling. If we may put a spin on that, Scripture seems to say we should work it out with fear and trembling because our souls are at stake, because God is working in us to perform his will. We dare not lessen that meaning, but perhaps we might add that in working out our salvation, we are called to do so with fear and trembling and not with timidity, cost-effectiveness, or stupidity. In short, a key problem with the fad and the faith is often the process rather than the desire for improvement. That is to say: to desire to make how we do the faith better is not a terrible thing, but how often is the proposed New Thing a way to avoid hard truth, hard teachings, the disciplines? God lends us the freedom to attempt change and growth, but how frequently are those attempts brought through a thoughtful, discerning, evaluative process?

Tools for Discernment

Discerning if a proposed change is about improvement, or an exercise in vanity, can be difficult. Fortunately, there are tools for discernment available to the believer. Some of these are of a spiritual nature: Scripture, prayer, humility, your church family, and the Holy Spirit. Other tools include those with which God has blessed all human beings: reflection, intelligence, compassion, reason.

The Role of Scripture

Discernment: for him who has ears to hear. We all desire to have insight and also to understand. Or do we? Discernment is something, we are told, is to be fervently prayed for. Writes Paul, "And this is my prayer: that your love may abound more and more in knowledge and depth of insight, so that you may be able to discern what is best and may be pure and blameless for the day of Christ"

(Phil 1:9–10). After one, a committee, or a congregation, decides to actually begin some deliberative thought, what specifics might be considered before the adoption of, say, a new style of music, before the publication of a novel, before ground is broken on a church building? What follows is a basic list of some convictions we know from the faith, from Scripture, most of which are either obvious or at least typically not contentious. This is not meant to be an exhaustive list, but it may provide a good starting point when considering *the next move*. We think of them as bricks of the faith and contend that when those start to be removed, edifices may crumble.

Christianity Is Hard

Christian living is not a matter of convenience. Christ said that if we want to follow, we must take up our cross daily and follow him. (Note, not just take it up and wander aimlessly about.) We are also told by Christ that narrow is the path to salvation, wide that to destruction. We may debate if that is or is not about salvation but, at the very least, it seems to tell us something important about what it means to be a Christian disciple in this life. Is this New Thing attempting to dodge the hard truth about Christian living? Does it gloss over what it means to give ourselves, all of our self, to Christ? Readers are reminded of the statement by Michael Ramsden in chapter 4: "I'm not aware of any effective model for discipleship in the church of Jesus Christ that doesn't cost everything."[6] Have we, in the West, developed models more in regard to values that drive fads rather than with reflection upon what is actually demanded for followers of Christ?

---

6. Ramsden, "Michael Ramsden Q&A." A good discussion of why Christian ethics do not only apply when convenient can be had by watching Michael Ramsden's other lecture, *Calling the Humanist Bluff*. He reminds us that the parable of the Good Samaritan was not about convenience but about the call to lay down our life.

Jesus Said His Yoke Was Light, His Burden Easy

Rather the flip-side of the above: Does the New Thing make it too hard, demand of us more than what Scripture demands? Perhaps the most obvious example of this, and an insidious and perennial problem, is teaching that leads to a works-based salvation. We all know, perhaps first hand, the cruel guilt of that road. If the New Thing teaches an expectation that we need to do something that may indicate a less-than-fine path to tread. We hope it is obvious that Christians do actually need to do things, that we are the hands and feet of Christ, that we are, for example, to love our neighbors, return good for evil, and make disciples. But sometimes fads come along that promote too much doing and for the wrong reasons.[7]

The World Will, at One Time or Another, Hate Us

Jesus said, "If the world hates you, keep in mind that it hated me first. If you belonged to the world, it would love you as its own. As it is, you do not belong to the world, but I have chosen you out of the world. That is why the world hates you" (John 15:18–19), and in Matthew 10 Jesus said:

> I am sending you out like sheep among wolves. Therefore, be as shrewd as snakes and as innocent as doves. Be on your guard; you will be handed over to the local councils and be flogged in the synagogues. On my account, you will be brought before governors and kings as witnesses to them and to the Gentiles. But when they arrest you, do not worry about what to say or how to say it. At that time you will be given what to say, for it will not be you speaking, but the Spirit of your Father speaking through you. Brother will betray brother to death,

7. We may consider the relatively new preoccupation some Christians have taken with Jewish/Hebraic ritual and custom. When is it learning about the world in which Jesus lived and taught and when does that degrade into a subtle intrusion of works theology, a preening self-righteousness, or at the least, a waste of time?

and a father his child; children will rebel against their
parents and have them put to death. You will be hated by
everyone because of me, but the one who stands firm to
the end will be saved. (Matt 10:16–22)

Oh, what a shame that the early church did not have the benefit of
laser shows, smoke machines, and badly done drama. That would
have stopped the world from hating the church. A critical question to be asked before the New Thing is adopted: Does it, in one
manner or another, attempt to water that truth, that the world will
hate followers of Christ, down? Does it attempt to make the world
love us? Surely one way to consider the popular "seeker friendly"
churches and services is as an attempt to have the world like us
more, to offer a version of Christianity, or Christian worship, that
is more appealing, more engaging, more entertaining. To be sure,
it is difficult and unpleasant to come to terms with this basic fact of
the faith: the world is at odds with Christ. If we identify and follow
Christ, we will be at odds with the world, and that is a tough place
to be. But it is where all Christians are called to be and to remain.
We are called to be faithful to Jesus, not merely to make nice and
be attractive and appealing. We might usefully recall here that the
Christian mission is not to make Christianity something it is not,
nor to present a kinder, gentler, easier Christianity; our mission is
to preach the Good News and to make disciples. It is to the God
of truth, wisdom, love, and mercy we point, and not our own attempts to be friendly and attractive.

There Is an Evil Tempter Working to Distort, Distract, and Thwart Any Attempt to Better Understand or Perceive or Carry Out the Duties of a Christian

In Colossians, we are directed by Paul time and again back to
Christ, and to seek all the treasures there. He writes, "I say this in
order that no one may mislead and delude you by plausible and
persuasive and attractive arguments and beguiling speech" (Col
2:4 AMP). But who could possibly mislead us? We must never

forget Screwtape roams the earth seeking to destroy. *Beguiled* is not a difficult state to fall into.

The Earth God Made Is Good, but It Is Broken

Everything in it is broken. Everyone in it is broken. We are corrupt and sinful creatures. Our motives can *always* be challenged. Our motives ought always be challenged when proposing some change. We should be willing and open for that challenge. Mature Christians should know it is good to have someone scratch at our motives and our reasons. Making all of this all the more difficult, of course, is when we remember that there is an evil tempter working to distort, distract, and thwart any attempt to better understand or perceive or carry out the duties of a Christian. Of particular danger is any attempt towards a utopian solution, any thinking that *this change will fix everything*. In our critique of the culture, Guinness says:

> We must each follow our calling, pursue our utmost for his highest in every possible way and count unquestioningly on the dynamics of the kingdom of God, and then knowing our own chronic ignorance and the probable incompleteness of our endeavors, trust the outcomes to God.[8]

Utopianism is a perennial temptation, for the Christian (and for the non-Christian, but believers understand why it is so for them). The Social Gospel movement, mentioned in chapter 1, was utopian, assumed it would bring in the millennial rule of Christ, and fix everything. On a much smaller scale, how many attempts at change are "for the better" when "better" has not been discussed?

Pride, Pride, Pride

See most of this section and most of the Bible.

8. Guinness, *Renaissance*, 112.

We Are on the Winning Team

This is so obvious that it hides in plain sight, but it needs restating. Christians win, or perhaps more appropriately stated: Christ wins. He has won. We do not win by anything we have done, what we may do, but by what has been done for us. But since we are on the winning team, might that put our activities here on earth into a different perspective? It strikes us that Christians play for the long game. We get that this life is filled with pain and suffering and that it will end. In some ways, the most essential metaphor for Christians is the tortoise and the hare. The fast game is very much an obsession with the fad. What matters is what we have at this moment, success, wealth, and fame. For Christians in the long game, however, we see the superficiality of those things. We know they are fleeting. We keep them in perspective. What matters more than all of that, and what puts any earthly glories into their right place, is knowing we are on the winning team. It is done. Your team wins. And it is the greatest win in all of history because the win is forever.

Life Is but a Vapor

Naturally, Americans are oblivious to the fact that we will actually, really, someday die. No, that happens to others, those who are not as healthy, not as devout. Weirdly obvious, perhaps the most obvious, certainly the most assured human event, but one that gets ignored, is the inevitability of death. Life is but a vapor. Everything and everyone will pass. Everything. We don't like to think about this. Nothing in this life lasts forever. Not our cars, not our families, our friends, our churches, denominations, nations, empires. Physics teaches that even the universe itself is running down. Where does this leave us and our (frequently) petty battles and issues and ideas? Do we ponder this weighty ultimate issue when considering making changes at church? Are they changes that, for example, might attempt to dull the horror of this vapor? Do we put death away, whisper about it in corners, or do we face it with courage, like grown-up men and women? Notably, some of our Christian ancestors desired to make grand works that demonstrated not the vapor, but the hope of eternity. They constructed massive, overwhelming works of permanent materials, stone, brick, lead, rising into the heavens. These are works that echo the endless joy of heaven and manifest a particular beauty that attracts even those who do not follow Christ. Perhaps something may be learned from their efforts.

No Man Knows the Hour

On the other hand, we can hear talk about millennialism, about Jesus' imminent return, about the rapture, and often it is a fad. We are told, very clearly, that there will be rumors and signs, but also that Christ's return will be "as a thief in the night" (Rev 16:15). So how do we live? We are to know that Christ could return any moment, but also that he has put us on this earth for, since his time here, two thousand years. A useful question might be: Would you live your life differently if you knew that Christ was not returning for, say, five hundred years? What might change? Why?

Winsome?

Paul writes:

> Though I am free and belong to no one, I have made myself a slave to everyone, to win as many as possible. To the Jews I became like a Jew, to win the Jews. To those under the law I became like one under the law (though I myself am not under the law), so as to win those under the law. To those not having the law I became like one not having the law (though I am not free from God's law but am under Christ's law), so as to win those not having the law. To the weak I became weak, to win the weak. I have become all things to all people so that by all possible means I might save some. I do all this for the sake of the gospel, that I may share in its blessings. (1 Cor 19–23)

A particularly potent bit of gospel for Americans as we, too, are free. Do we seek to make ourselves slaves to everyone? Anyone? More to the point: Is the New Thing one that will help us in the church to become slaves so as to win the weak, to save some, all for the sake of the gospel? Might the New Thing be one that is attractive, and attractive not merely aesthetically but in a sense enriching, invigorating, meaningful, hopeful? We seek not merely to fill the pews but to be, and make, disciples. Is the New Thing set to appropriately woo people to Christ?

Growth

We know we are supposed to be growing. What does that mean? How a fellowship defines this carries many implications. Does growth mean more people attending, more money towards projects, more funds for charity, or more fruits of the Spirit? It seems obvious when put in the list above, yet we somehow often forget which growth is the priority. If we, our fellowship, are not growing in fruit, not growing in obedience, does much else matter? In some ways, this is the core of the fad problem: we know that we need to grow in the meaningful ways, and we know that means work, discipline, time, and quietness. (If you don't yet know this, please re-read most of the New Testament.) When a suggestion comes down the pike that promises more growth, or, say, a more efficient, simpler, faster, cheaper means to grow, well, it is easy to buy it (in both senses). Perhaps asking the simple questions will direct us to the appropriate answer. Will the New Thing produce in me, or in others to whom I need to minister, more discipline, more willingness to obey what Christ taught, more selfless behavior? If not, maybe a time to reconsider just what it is that you are prioritizing. "If you will here stop and ask yourselves why you are not as pious as the primitive Christians were, writes Law, "your own heart will tell you, that it is neither through ignorance nor inability, but purely because you never thoroughly intended it."[9]

9. Law, *A Serious Call.* If you do not know this book, you need to.

The Holy Spirit

Either the Spirit does, or does not, guide and direct and inspire. We sometimes think this is the most difficult struggle for Christians. We all desperately want the Spirit to guide and instruct, we want that confirmation, affirmation, and inspiration, but something breaks down. Perhaps our culturally conditional scientific rationalism just gets the better of us. Perhaps we do not know how to unleash, so to speak, the Spirit. Or perhaps we expect the Spirit operates in much the same way as fads: we want the Spirit to tell us all the answers, to make all the good things happen, before we have actually gone and done any of the good, hard work. And we "know" the Spirit is working when we *feel* a certain way. No. As with many of the other problems of the fad, contemporary Christians are also affected by the culture and its relentless selling of "I feel that . . . " Of course, the Christian way of selling that is by saying, "The Spirit told me to . . . " Philip Carey points out that Solomon desired wisdom, but knew that was not gained by a short-cut: "He doesn't believe in magic potions or recipes or fruit that could make him wise with one bite. He wants the real thing, which means it must be his own heart that is shaped in wisdom by the Spirit of the Lord; he's going to have to learn."[10]

How would we know if it is the Spirit directing us towards the New Thing, or not? We would ask others, subject it to Scripture, subject it to reasonability, *et al.* There seems an order here: Do we seek our own understanding and judgment first, or God's? Can we say with Spurgeon, "The counsel of the infallible God I seek in preference to my own judgment or the advice of friends"?[11]

---

10. Carey, *Good News for Anxious Christians*, 75. Cary covers a good many topics and we highly recommend his book. He nails an issue related to the fad when discussing "Consumerist Christianity."

11. Spurgeon, *Faith's Checkbook.*

The Role of Reason

What was discussed in the previous section is considering if a recommended change, a new fad, a proposed program, is more or less scriptural or if it is accurate to biblical teaching. In many ways, we may think of this as simply a comparison, indeed, a rational comparison, between what Scripture says and what the New Thing may offer. It is our attempt to hold the New Thing to a standard, to discern if it measures up. This is one manner in which Christians attempt to discern.

Another manner in which humans try to discern direction is a gift that all humans have available to them: reason. God provided this to all humans. It is of profound significance as it enables us to get distance from ourselves. Reason is a way to move past mere passions and desires, to grasp at the *thing* out there, something I have a choice about engaging with. It can be pursued with means other than my own preferences. People who believe in reason believe that we can act more, or less, rationally. Engagement with the world can be about something other than me. This is also one of the paths towards salvation—we recognize it is not all about us, that there is something beyond our desires, a reason, if you will, for our entire life.

But reason itself can quickly turn sticky for the Christian; indeed, for all humans. We tend to think, particularly in the West, that being reasonable, rational, logical (and they are not all the same thing), leads to better outcomes. Generally speaking, we may be hard pressed to disagree with that, and yet, we also know that horrendous evil has been pursued because someone thought it reasonable. Sometime we may use reason to sort out that something else is unreasonable, but more to the point, reason must have a direction, an end, a grounding. Consider this analysis of the trap of reason in regard to what must surely be now considered a Christian fad, one with disastrous consequences: eighteenth-century deism. Writes Willey: "The strength of deism, as of every kind of modernism, lay in its determination to have no grounds for its belief of which were not absolutely firm and sure. Its weakness lay in its too facile assumption that it had found such grounds." And he continues, "God never intended us to have any knowledge so clear and certain as to leave nothing for faith to exercise itself upon. Just as in everyday affairs we often have to act upon probability rather than certainty, so in religion our faith must often rest upon evidence which falls short of demonstration."[12] Followers of Christ are instructed to follow him first, not our reason, not our passions. Putting it a slightly different way: following Christ means putting what he wants above both our human passions and our human reason, yet human reason remains a valuable tool when, like all tools, it is wielded correctly.

Cost

To begin, here we mean actual fiscal considerations, not abstract "costs" as in freedom or time or lives. Quite stunningly, and perhaps most amazing of all the issues in this book, are the ways in which Christians can be undeniably, obviously, and utterly bizarre with spending. Please consider for a moment not how this works in your church but how you think about money in your own life, your own family. What does it mean to be fiscally responsible? This appears to be a struggle for most Americans: check the level of debt held currently by Americans. (A quick Google search reveals much.) It is not good, there is a lot of debt. If you do not understand that debt is bad, that what it does to your income is bad, please do another Google search to read about the effects. Of course, in the same ways debt is bad for a family, debt is bad for a church. When the New Thing is being considered, the financial costs involved need to be laid out clearly and thoughtfully. Like with any other decision that involves borrowing money, the same steps ought occur.

12. Willey, *Christianity Past and Present*, 99. The quote concludes, "Revelation may not be as free from anomalies as we should have liked, or thought appropriate, but (as Butler said) 'he who denies the Scripture to have been from God on account of these difficulties, may, for the very same reason, deny the world to have been formed by Him.'"

Then there are the other costs, the human costs. This too seems an area that requires careful consideration. Following Christ means a profound cost to ourselves: everything. And this, of course, and as is well known, may also mean our life. We understand this as something that may be required of us. But there is also the sort of human cost in regard to taking advantage of others. For example, perhaps your church has adopted a New Thing that is some sort of program, something that requires staffing. Is that cost being appropriately considered? While we all recognize that our very lives are to be dutifully held up to God, it is not our role to assume we can request the same of others.

Means for Ends

Perhaps for those who do not follow Christ it may make a kind of sense in that means *are* the only ends. When the transcendent is denied, what ends might there be? For the Christian, this is never appropriate or desirable. There is only one end and to miss that end is to miss everything. In C.S. Lewis's, *The Great Divorce*, some of the most insightful and convicting moments are when the individuals who are in Heaven for a day trip cannot discern, even when in front of them, that they have sought the wrong ends. One character, a clergyman, enjoyed great success on earth; when confronted directly and bluntly with his apostasy, he brushes it off, chides the accuser for name calling, and is concerned about the next meeting in Hell wherein really deep theological issues will be addressed. When suggesting or evaluating a proposed change, of course, we must consider: By what criteria do we deem it good? Does it advance an end? Surely for the Christian it must, at all costs, refrain from seeking an end other than the love of God and obedience to him. Wrote George MacDonald:

> If you who set yourselves to explain the theory for Christianity, had set yourselves instead to do the will of the Master, the one object for which the gospel was preached to you, how different would now be the condition of that portion of the world with which you come into contact!

Had you given yourselves to the understanding of his word that you might do it, and not to the quarrying from it of material wherewith to buttress your systems, in many a heart by this time would the name of the Lord be loved where now it remains unknown.[13]

Not about You. No, Seriously, It Is Not about You.

"You just aren't that special."

—DUSTY RUSH, MY PASTOR

Would you do half of the activities you currently do, writing, singing, painting, lecturing, preaching, helping, if you knew ahead of time there wasn't any chance for recognition of any kind? Would it make a difference in your goals if you signed everything you did with a pseudonym? For many years in the church, it was typical practice for ministers and choirs to wear robes. This was, at least at the start, not a way of flaunting something at church but a means of depersonalizing or covering up what was superficial and focusing on what was to be happening during worship.

As some of the examples in this book have made obvious, fads can lead to desiring "special" knowledge as well as "special" ability or "insight." With that may follow fame and fortune. In a commercial culture, the new reigns and rewards follow. Christians ought to be suspicious of such; our goals do not include being up-to-date with the latest New Thing, but rather with obedience, service, and taking up our crosses daily.

Some Christians are indeed doing just that. Hard to say if those sorts of believers purposefully seek out anonymity. We suspect that if asked what they are trying to make others think about them, the anonymous Christian would reply that they are not thinking about themselves at all. Where are those folks who are keeping under the radar, those who are not much noticed? Well, they are hard to find. They do not do the glamorous work; they are

13. MacDonald, *Creation in Christ*, 102.

not the face of any organization. They are probably the ones who clean the toilets at church or spending afternoons with terminally ill or the tragically lonely. What they do typically does not garner headlines, in or out of church. They live quiet lives of sacrifice; they do not seek out excitement, fame, or notice. The virtue of their lives challenge us to ask: What am I seeking?

Boredom and Originality

How would it be if you learned that from now on you would only be permitted a single change of clothing, a single set, that when it wore out would be replaced by a similar set? But why should it matter? How many millions are spent each year to update home kitchens, not merely for a functionally better stove and fridge but for appearance? So we update. We update everything, all the time, and we tend to judge others who do not keep up. Fashion, fads, and trends all play a role and, as this book has aspired to demonstrate, often this is to a ludicrous and thoughtless degree. However, it clearly is possible to talk about how, for example, new clothes may enrich our lives. (A new suit when a man is released from prison is not meaningless.) For the Christian, we know that "all things are made new," and often the material manifestations of that can be reminders and can bring a measure of happiness and thankfulness.

But we might also consider that typically the issue comes down to a sort of boredom. How often have we heard, "I find the music at church boring." Or less heard, but maybe more thought: "The sermons are boring." When is the problem with practices and environments being actually boring and when is the problem us? Boredom is generally about me, my desires and wants. If I am growing bored, is it because I am not doing what I ought to be doing? Consider boredom in the context of what Paul wrote to the Ephesians, "Be very careful, then, how you live, not as unwise but as wise, making the most of every opportunity, because the days are evil. Therefore do not be foolish, but understand what the Lord's will is" (Eph 5:15–17).

A related means to assess the New Thing, and our motives for adopting it, is to consider how much of it is dedicated to being original or "fresh" or "new." Irving Babbitt, commenting on the change in western art, stated: "The chief ambition of our modern art, which resembles in this respect some of the art of the later Renaissance, is to be original. The first aim of both classic and neo-classic art, on the other hand, was to be representative."[14] A hallmark, if not obsession of at least the last two centuries of western civilization has been the cult of originality, if the fine arts are any measure. We are hard-pressed to think Duchamp's *Fountain*, an upside-down urinal, a qualitative advance, but it certainly was original. There are examples within Christendom to answer the relentless press for originality. Basilican-planned churches have not changed much since the fourth century. The Gothic style has been revived several times. In the Orthodox tradition, icons have been painted the same for a thousand years.

C.S. Lewis commented that the method of modern literature might be a problem for Christians. There was a "repugnance of atmospheres, a discordance of notes, an incompatibility of temperaments." Why? Because (comments Lewis ironically) "Great authors are innovators, pioneers, explorers; bad authors bunch in schools and follow models . . . great authors are always 'breaking fetters' and 'bursting bonds.'"[15] How much might a desire for the original be driving the New Thing? Does love, the expression of love, go out of fashion, become old and hackneyed? Is a pursuit for the new leading us to neglect charity, mercy, humility? Lewis also suggested, "And always, of every idea and of every method he will ask not, 'Is it mine?' but, 'Is it good?'"[16]

---

14. Babbitt, *Literature and the American College*, 220.

15. Lewis, "Christianity and Literature," in *Essay Collection*, 413.

16. Lewis, "Christianity and Literature," 418.

Side-Effects

What does it mean if your New Thing is a wild success, or total failure? Are you ready to respond rightly in either event? Are you, or the group, willing and able to see the New Thing die and go away? It may be worth contemplating how you would respond should someone affected by the New Thing complains that it is wrong or silly. How might you respond?

Considering Together

One of the most important steps that can be taken when considering the New Thing is to actually *consider* it. Consideration ought to be in the same manner in which believers make any decisions, changes or adaptations. In all our congregations, and indeed our own lives, we need to thoughtfully, prayerfully, and carefully consider changes. In this consideration, this process, there are important roles for many to undertake, roles of elders, leadership, community, family, friends. Do we ever even stop to request they listen to our plans, to give us their opinions, to pray for our endeavors?

Two examples may shed light on how far away from this we have moved. The ministry of musician Keith Green during the 70s made, and promoted, many innovative changes. What we take as a thoughtful attempt to negotiate the new was how those involved in the ministry prayed. Groups of brothers and sisters were designated to commit themselves to praying during recording sessions. Another example comes from ancient history. During the early church, as Christians were finding their way, a young man joined and was faced with a dilemma. He was an actor, in the Roman theatre, an environment that was decadent. He approached the elders of his church and asked them what he should do—a particularly important matter as it concerned his livelihood. The elders told him they would pray. A few weeks later, they met with him, told him they thought it best if he left the theatre, and said that the church would support him while he attempted to find other work.[17]

What else may our brothers and sisters at church do to assist consideration of the New Thing? An uncomfortable, but perhaps necessary function, is for those to whom we are accountable to question motives. What is at work, or may be at work, in regard to motives for the New Thing? Vanity? Self-deception? Fear? And here we can perhaps see the difference clearly. What ought to be behind any change, program, or adjustment that Christians make? A desire to reduce ourselves, love our neighbors, seek the truth, please God, remain obedient? We need those around us, those in our families and churches, to ask these questions, constantly, fervently. We cannot slip on this. If we do, and we forget, we end up with fads and, maybe worse, a vapid faith.

The Lord says:

> These people come near to me with their mouth
> and honor me with their lips,
> but their hearts are far from me.
> Their worship of me
> is based on merely human rules they have been taught.
> Therefore once more I will astound these people
> with wonder upon wonder;
> the wisdom of the wise will perish,
> the intelligence of the intelligent will vanish. (Isa 29:13–14)

Considering the New Thing

One of the difficulties of this entire process, of knowing if we should adopt the New Thing, is what is even meant by innovation, progress, growth, or development? Do we have any idea what Christian growth should look like? (Maybe not because it happens so infrequently?) Do we have a clear idea as to what growth should look like in our ministries? Churches? Do we even have a clear and

17. For this story I am indebted to Bercot, *The Kingdom that Turned the World Upside Down*. We find it notable that they did not say to their brother, "What a great opportunity for you to minister to actors!"

thoughtful understanding as to what progress (if that is the word) looks like in regard to our very own Christian life?

In *The Abolition of Man*, C.S. Lewis discussed one example of what a good advance may look like. He suggests that there was a genuine advance, improvement, from the Silver Rule of Confucius, "Do not do unto others as you would not wish them to do to you" to the Golden Rule of Christianity, "Do unto others as you would have them do unto you." We can see this not as an innovation but as an advance of the same principle.[18] This marks an improvement, not a new ethic; not merely a change, but real progress. To be asked for any New Thing: Does the innovation advance a principle or try to create a new one?

Seeking the Eternal

What attracts and repels the world away from Christ and from his church? The same things that have been attractive since Jesus walked the earth: love, joy, peace, hope, compassion, mercy. Is this how we attempt to become attractive today? Here is one distinction: we desire (or should) to be attractive in substance. We do not need to seek to be attractive in style. Or, at least, that oughtn't to be our first concern. When we concern ourselves with being attractive, stylistically, that seems a weak path. If we happen to be so, fine, but why seek that first rather than the substantial?

What does it mean to be attractive in substance? We suggest it has to do with the perennial attractiveness, and satisfaction, of seeking and finding wisdom. Clearly, one of the goals of the Christian is to avoid the transitory and to seek the eternal, the lasting, and the divine. Notably, this has also been the goal of many other cultures: Greeks sought the Ideal, Confucians the Way. Even

18. Lewis, *Abolition of Man*, 57. Lewis continues here, comparing the idea of innovation to Nietzsche: "Nietzsche's ethic is an innovation, that is, an attempt at something totally new where traditional morality is rejected along with the foundation for any value whatsoever. A genuine advance is like someone who loves fresh vegetables and decides to grow their own rather than purchase them at the store. An innovation would mean rejecting vegetables totally and trying to eat bricks and centipedes."

science, in a related way, seeks that which is most accurate most of the time and not subject to opinion. Paul writes, "Since we consider and look not to the things that are seen but to the things that are unseen; for the things that are visible are temporal (brief and fleeting), but the things that are invisible are deathless and everlasting" (2 Cor 4:18 AMP). Why do we look to those things? Because we seek wisdom, and wisdom does not dwell in the realm of the fad.

Reflecting the Truth

Christians believe there are answers, and that they are perennial and universal; that is, they are the sorts of questions that all humans ask themselves, and have asked, since humanity was capable of self-reflection. A problem in regard to knowledge and answers that Christians and non-Christians both face is how to negotiate that space wherein we have confidence in our knowledge but are also open to learning. Delsol puts this issue quite well:

> He knows he is neither justice nor liberty, but rather a servant, inadequate and unguided, of their realization, which is never fully known. He errs on the side of making adjustments, because he is always inadequate for the causes he defends. His judgments and acts are inspired by the referent, which he can never quite grasp in its entirety. He belongs to the truth. The truth does not belong to him but exudes from every part of him.[19]

Or to put it another way, now we see but through a glass darkly. Christians know the truth is not *them*, not their thoughts; the truth is Christ. We aspire for glimpses of that knowledge, of the

19. Delsol, *The Unlearned Lessons*, 105. Delsol's book is not arguing for the faith but rather against skepticism and fanaticism. She grasps that humans must have a place to stand, a place not of their own invention, but a place that permits freedom and the ability, as she puts it, to become a subject. Hopefully it is obvious that her quote rather parallels the Christian situation. We are to be not merely hearers, but doers of the word. The rest of her book contains excellent criticisms of modern thinking but, alas, not a terrific answer for where to turn. We wish she could look more closely at the faith.

wisdom, of that divine beauty. The Christian method of negotiat-
ing the uneasy space between assurance in our knowledge and an
open mind, between faith and reason, recognizes that that gap can
be a place for growth.

That is all well and good when we live among a group of
people who are all attempting to seek wisdom, to find a truth not
them. What happens, however, when those who look towards an
ontological realm live in a culture where the idea of anything beyond the personal is received with skepticism? Well, it is tough. Ultimately, the problem of the fad, and its related cult of originality,
spring from a profound misunderstanding of truth. Wrote Isaiah
Berlin, "[N]o one today is surprised by the assumption that variety
is, in general, preferable to uniformity—monotony uniformity, are
pejorative" and he concludes by pointing to "the notion that One
is good, Many—diversity—is bad, since the truth is one, and only
error is multiple, is far older . . . "[20] Perhaps an oversimplification,
but when the transcendent is denied, what remains but the error of
the multiple will? Another oversimplification has been the materi-
alist story of the West, that with enough science, over enough time,
humanity will improve. Molnar notes that modernist utopians be-
lieved that after collecting facts and rationally organizing them,
mankind could be perfected.[21] With those two, rejection of any

20. Berlin, *The Crooked Timber of Humanity*, 207. His complete quote is
instructive in that it seems to connect modernist materialism to the postmodern will: "[N]o one today is surprised by the assumption that variety is,
in general, preferable to uniformity—monotony uniformity, are pejorative
words—or, to turn to qualities of character, that integrity and sincerity are
admirable independently of the truth of validity of the beliefs or principles
involved; that warm-hearted idealism is nobler, if less expedient, than cold
realism; or tolerance than intolerance, even though these virtues can be taken
too far and lead to dangerous consequences; and so on. Yet this has not long
been so; for the notion that One is good, Many—diversity—is bad, since the
truth is one, and only error is multiple, is far older, and deeply rooted in the
Platonic tradition." In the following paragraph Berlin writes, "[W]hat Catholic
in . . . the sixteenth century would say, 'I abhor the heresies of the reformers,
but I am deeply moved by the sincerity and integrity with which they hold
and practice and sacrifice themselves for their abominable beliefs." Berlin, *The
Crooked Timber of Humanity*, 207.

21. Molnar, *Utopia*, 91.

transcendent at which to aim our life and the utter belief that given enough time Utopia will emerge, a culture cannot be other than fad driven. Christians, on the other hand, seek something quite different. As Richard Weaver wrote not long ago:

> The believer in truth, on the other hand, is bound to maintain that the things of highest value are not affected by the passage of time; otherwise the very concept of truth becomes impossible. In declaring that we wish to recover lost ideals and values, we are looking toward an ontological realm, which is timeless.[22]

There are traps at every turn: if we go one direction we risk sacrificing the truth for the fad, for comfort, for fame; if we go the other, we risk entrenching ourselves in stifling tradition, dead ritual, and a faith that provides little for life now. How then ought the believer to decide, to choose, to live? Because we know the truth is not us, not made by humankind, we can grasp that while some of the truth is knowable, and that all ought to seek it, none has a monopoly on it. Warner suggests a sort of balance:

> Of course we all make ridiculous mental reservations for the sake of what we value and love. The old tradition-weighted forms and ceremonies come down to us through the centuries mellowed by the spirits of countless high and humble saints, and we worship God best somehow by means of them. And yet we must ride loose, I am certain. The question above all questions we must ask ourselves is "IS IT TRUE," not "Does it help me?" We need not fear about the second question if we stand by the first.[23]

---

22. Weaver, *Ideas Have Consequences*, 52.
23. Warner, *Hugh Compton Warner*, 61.

The Truth, the Mirror, and the Glass

Lewis suggested a mirror metaphor.[24] That is, we are to not show our own faces but to reflect Christ's. Certainly, this is one manner we may consider the actions of our Christian lives. Another may be that we are to act like lenses. We focus on Christ and aspire to make him sharper, clearer, more easily seen for others. Our job is to be clear and permit the light to shine through. We are to be sure and polish the lenses as best we can and to keep moving the lenses so as to keep the truth in focus. Will the New Thing accomplish, in some way, maintaining a focus on Christ, keeping the truth sharp, polishing the lenses for clarity, or will it clutter and distract?

The Innovator and the Master

> Virtue cannot be simply passed on as a form of abstract knowledge; rather, the way to learn virtue is to observe the virtuous man and imitate him, building up the habits of right judgment and right action. Once virtue is understood in this way, the folly of the sophists is revealed. One cannot buy a habit or purchase experience, any more than one can buy a ready-made ditch. It takes time and effort to build character. It cannot be bought, sold, seized, or clutched. To attain virtue, one must find a worthy guide, and sit at his feet as a student, a *discipulus*. One must find a *magister*—not just a teacher, but a master.[25]

Remember the Elon Musk story, the brave crusading creator who, against all odds, turns out to know better than the stuck-in-the-mud Old Timers? It turns out there is another story that we are fond of, one that, notably, is rather the antithesis of the Underdog/paradigm shift/cutting edge tale. We very much like the Master Craftsman Story. What do we expect of a Master Craftsman? Do we expect originality and flash? Why do we hold the Master

---

24. Lewis suggests this in different places. See, *The Four Loves*, 180, or the essay mentioned above, "Christianity and Literature," 416.

25. Senz, "Buying Virtue."

Craftsman in high regard? Because they can entertain us? What is the difference between a Master and an Innovator? Part of it has to do with seeing what works and what does not.

Imitation is done in the hope of reaching betterment. This is the wee gray-haired gent who, sitting at his workshop table, night after night, has become expert in the fabrication of hand-made shoes just as his father before him, and he before him. Or perhaps the Orthodox monks who paint small icon portraits with the same materials and techniques that have been used to make them for more than a thousand years. Or perhaps making instruments, like Antonio Stradivari, the brilliant (notice how that word works when used with the Master Story) violin-maker. George Eliot ponders what it meant for Stradivari to have such skill. In her poem, *Antonio*, she presents the Master, Antonio, as considering his creative skills from God and what that means. At the end of the poem, a critic exclaims that a rival violin-maker, Giuseppe, crafts violins just as popular and as good as the Master's, to which the Master replies:

> May be: they are different.
> His quality declines: he spoils his hand
> With over-drinking. But were his the best,
> He could not work for two. My work is mine,
> And, heresy or not, if my hand slacked
> I should rob God—since his is fullest good—
> Leaving a blank instead of violins.
> I say, not God himself can make man's best
> Without best men to help him.
>
> 'Tis God gives skill,
> But not without men's hands: he could not make
> Antonio Stradivari's violins
> Without Antonio. Get thee to thy easel.

How do we describe what a Master does? It is not innovation, it is rather a sort of seeking to improve, to perfect. We may be reminded to be "perfect, therefore, as your heavenly Father is perfect" (Matt 6:48). The idea here is that perfection, completeness, is sought, pursued. Which model seeks perfection, the ideal, the complete, the Innovator or the Master? We call men like Elon Musk daring innovators. We call men like Antonio, Master. Jesus, too, we call Master. At which story ought we to aim our Christian life?

I tell you that this man, rather than the other, went home justified before God. For all those who exalt themselves will be humbled, and those who humble themselves will be exalted.

—LUKE 18:14

Appendix I

Questions for Innovators
Hoping to Avoid Faddism

WHEN CONSIDERING A CHANGE, an adaption, use, or the New Thing, the following questions may help to sharpen debate:

- Will this, in any way, bring shame to the name of Jesus?

- Does it honor Christ?

- Is this about me? At all? No, seriously, it is about me or God?

- Am I excited about this project/song/book/lesson/sermon/poem because it will "make others really get it!" or because it will more clearly point to Christ?

- Have I submitted my idea to those I respect spiritually, perhaps elders at church, and asked what they think?

- Will it help others with humility, charity, forgiveness, hope, discernment, and love?

- How much of this has to do with selling books (or selling anything)?

- Do I assume I have a better handle than, say, *everyone* else on this particular fine point of doctrine, practice, liturgy, and spirituality?

Appendix I

- Even if I do not have all the answers, and I do not, is it valuable to address this issue? Can I say why? Can I explain why it matters to engage thinking and conversation about this issue?

- How do I actively avoid having any of this reflect upon me?

- Does this New Thing inflate my ego?

- How does this New Thing contribute to the Kingdom?

- Does it assist in encouraging the brothers and sisters at church?

- Does it assist in producing Kingdom fruit? Does it produce love and peace?

- Do I think I have all the answers when others do not?

- Does this unite or divide? Accurately?

- Does it assist in apologizing for (i.e., defending) the gospel?

- Am I sure this has not been done before? Does that matter? Have I studied history enough to know if something like this was tried before? And failed?

- Is this something that I am being led to promulgate? Is the Spirit involved in it?

- Is it going to bring glory to God?

- Might the manner in which this is done, the style in this thing I am trying to do, carry with it a particular meaning all its own? Is that dangerous?

- Would I do this if I knew I would get no remuneration, no fame, no praise, no glory?

- What would my grandmother think about this?

- Would my grandmother do this?

- What would Jesus think about this project or activity?

- Would Jesus do this?

- Is this biblical?

- Is it rational?

- What is my response to criticism of my ideas?

Questions for Innovators Hoping to Avoid Faddism

- Will it in any way bring me honor and praise? Might that be a problem?

- If I do receive honor and praise for this, can I prepare myself to handle it?

- If I receive condemnation for this, am I prepared to handle that?

Appendix II

List of Resolutions
from Jonathan Edwards

IN 1722, JONATHAN EDWARDS started a list of resolutions. Perhaps hard to believe today, but this was at one time a not uncommon practice for college-aged men. We found them useful when considering the Christian life. We also found them profoundly humbling.

The following is a selection from his *70 Resolutions*.

Being sensible that I am unable to do anything without God's help, I do humbly entreat him by his grace to enable me to keep these Resolutions, so far as they are agreeable to his will, for Christ's sake.

REMEMBER TO READ OVER THESE RESOLUTIONS ONCE A WEEK.

1. Resolved, That I will do whatsoever I think to be most to the glory of God and my own good, profit, and pleasure, in the whole of my duration; without any consideration of the time, whether now or never so many myriads of ages hence. Resolved to do whatever I think to be my duty, and most for the good and advantage of mankind in general.

4. Resolved, Never to do any manner of thing, whether in soul or body, less or more, but what tends to the glory of God, nor be, nor suffer it, if I can possibly avoid it.

8. Resolved, To act, in all respects, both speaking and doing, as if nobody had been so vile as I, and as if I had committed the same sins, or had the same infirmities or failings as others; and that I will let the knowledge of their failings promote nothing but shame in myself, and prove only an occasion of my confessing my own sins and misery to God

12. Resolved, If I take delight in it as a gratification of pride, or vanity, or on any such account, immediately to throw it by.

13. Resolved, To be endeavouring to find out fit objects of charity and liberality.

17. Resolved, That I will live so, as I shall wish I had done when I come to die.

23. Resolved, Frequently to take some deliberate action, which seems most unlikely to be done, for the glory of God, and trace it back to the original intention, designs and ends of it; and if I find it not to be for God's glory, to repute it . . .

31. Resolved, Never to say anything at all against anybody, but when it is perfectly agreeable to the highest degree of Christian honour, and of love to mankind, agreeable to the lowest humility, and sense of my own faults and failings, and agreeable to the Golden Rule . . .

33. Resolved, To do, always, what I can towards making, maintaining and preserving peace, when it can be done without an overbalancing detriment in other respects.

34. Resolved, In narrations, never to speak anything but the pure and simple verity.

43. Resolved, Never, henceforth, till I die, to act as if I were in any way my own, but entirely and altogether God's.

44. Resolved, That no other end but religion, shall have any influence at all on any of my actions; and that no action shall be, in the least circumstance, any otherwise than the religious end will carry it.

45. Resolved, Never to allow any pleasure or grief, joy or sorrow, nor any affection at all, nor any degree of affection, nor any circumstance relating to it, but what helps Religion.

47. Resolved, To endeavour, to my utmost, to deny whatever is not most agreeable to a good and universally sweet and benevolent, quiet, peaceable, contented and easy, compassionate and generous, humble and meek, submissive and obliging, diligent and industrious, charitable and even, patient, moderate, forgiving and sincere, temper; and to do, at all times, what such a temper would lead me to do; and to examine strictly, at the end of every week, whether I have so done.

55. Resolved, To endeavour, to my utmost, so to act, as I can think I should do, if I had already seen the happiness of Heaven, and Hell torments.

58. Resolved, Not only to refrain from an air of dislike, fretfulness, and anger in conversation, but to exhibit an air of love, cheerfulness and benignity.

62. Resolved, Never to do anything but my duty, and then according to Eh. Vi, 6–8, to do it willingly and cheerfully, as unto the Lord, and not to men: knowing that whatever good thing any man doth, the same shall he receive of the Lord.

67. Resolved, After afflictions, to enquire, What I am the better for them; What good I have got by them; and, What I might have got by them.

Appendix III

Appendices and Fads

THIS APPENDIX IS INCLUDED as the next big thing in Christian publishing is sure to be lots of appendices.

Bibliography

Addams, Jane. *Tewenty Years at Hull-House*. Boston: Bedford/St. Martin's, 1999.

Ahlstrom, Sydney E. *A Religious History of the American People*. New Haven: Yale University Press, 1972.

Alnor, William M. *Heaven Can't Wait: A Survey of Alleged Trips to the Other Side*. Grand Rapids, MI: Baker, 1996.

Babbitt, Irving. *Literature and the American College: Essays in Defense of the Humanities*. Boston: Houghton, Mifflin & Co., 1908.

Baker, Paul. *Contemporary Christian Music: Where it came from What it is Where It's Going*. Wheaton, IL: Crossway, 1985.

Bartkowski, John. *The Promise Keepers: Servants, Soldiers, and Godly Men*. New Brunswick, NJ: Rutgers University Press, 2003.

Bateman, Bradley W. "The Social Gospel and the Progressive Era." *Divining America, TeacherServe, National Humanities Center* (blog). http://nationalhumanitiescenter.org/tserve/twenty/tkeyinfo/socgospel.htm.

Battle, John A. "A Brief History of the Social Gospel." *Western Reformed Seminary Journal* 6, no. x (1999) 5–11.

Bell, Rob. *What Is the Bible?: How an Ancient Library of Poems, Letters, and Stories Can Transform the Way You Think and Feel about Everything*. New York: HarperOne, 2017.

Bellemare, Marc. "Chronocentrism: 'This Time It's Different'." *Marc F. Bellemare: Agricultural and Applied Economics—Without Apology* (blog), November 21, 2011. http://marcfbellemare.com/wordpress/4744.

Bercot, David W. *The Kingdom That Turned the World Upside Down*. Amberson, PA: Scroll, 2009.

Berlin, Isaiah. *The Crooked Timber of Humanity*, edited by Henry Hardy. New York: Vintage, 1992.

Branaugh, Matt. "Willow Creek's 'Huge Shift': Influential megachurch moves away from seeker-sensitive services." *Christianity Today*, May 15, 2008. Accessed November 12, 2019. http://www.christianitytoday.com/ct/2008/june/5.13.html.

Carey, Phillip. *Good News for Anxious Christians: 10 Practical Things You Don't Have to Do*. Grand Rapids, MI: Brazos, 2010.

Bibliography

Carson, D.A. *Becoming Conversant with the Emerging Church: Understanding a Movement and Its Implications.* Grand Rapids, MI: Zondervan, 2005.

Delahoyde, Melinda. "Are Christians Headed for Disaster?" *Moody Monthly* 84 (1984) 18–20.

Delsol, Chantal. *The Unlearned Lessons of the Twentieth Century: An Essay on Late Modernity.* Translated by Robin Dick. Wilmington, DE: ISI, 2006.

"The Ever-Changing Fads of the Church." *Arminian Today* (blog), February 1, 2011. https://arminiantoday.wordpress.com/2011/02/01/the-ever-changing-fads-of-the-church/.

Flaubert, Gustave. *Madame Bovery.* Translated by Francis Steegmuller. New York: Random House, 1957.

Greek, Cecil E. *The Religious Roots of American Sociology.* New York: Garland, 1992.

Guinness, Os. *Renaissance: The Power of the Gospel However Dark the Times.* Downers Grove, IL: InterVarsity, 2014.

Hawkins, Greg, and Cally Parkinson. *Reveal: Where Are You?: The Answer Will Transform Your Church.* South Barrington, IL: Willow Creek Association, 2007.

Hobson, Theo. "Evangelicals Turning to Jewish Customs? It's Complicated." *The Guardian,* February 17, 2011. Accessed September 20, 2019. https://www.theguardian.com/commentisfree/belief/2011/feb/17/evangelical-christians-jewish-customs-judaism.

Huxley, Aldous. *Ends and Means: An Inquiry into the Nature of Ideals and into the Methods Employed for Their Realization.* New York: Harper & Brothers, 1937.

Kaiser, Menachem. "For Some Believers Trying to Connect with Jesus, the Answer Is to Live Like a Jew." *Tablet Magazine,* February 3, 2014. Accessed September 19, 2019. https://www.tabletmag.com/jewish-life-and-religion/161086/observing-torah-like-jesus.

Kershner, Irvin, dir. *Star Wars: The Empire Strikes Back.* 1980; San Rafael, CA: Twentieth Century Fox Home Entertainment, 2006. DVD.

Kilde, Jeanne Halgren. *When Church Became Theatre: The Transformation of Evangelical Architecture and Worship in Nineteenth-Century America.* Oxford: Oxford University Press, 2005.

Law, William. *A Serious Call to a Devout and Holy Life.* Alachua, FL: Bridge-Logos, 2008.

Lewis, C.S. *The Abolition of Man.* New York: Touchstone, 1996.

———. *Essay Collection & Other Short Pieces.* Edited by Lesley Walmsley. London: HarperCollins, 2000.

———. *The Discarded Image.* Cambridge: Cambridge University Press, 1964.

———. *The Four Loves.* London: Harcourt Brace Jovanovich, 1960.

———. *The Great Divorce.* London: Geoffrey Bles, 1945.

———. *The Screwtape Letters.* Ontario: Samizdat, 2016.

MacDonald, George. *Creation in Christ: Unspoken Sermons.* Edited by Rolland Hein. Vancouver, BC: Regent College Publishing, 1976.

Bibliography

Miller, Donald. *Blue Like Jazz: Non-Religious Thoughts on Christian Spirituality.* Nashville, TN: Thomas Nelson, 2003.

Molnar, Thomas. *The Future of Education.* New York: Fleet, 1961.

———. *Sartre: Ideologue of Our Time.* New York: Funk & Wagnalls, 1968.

———. *Utopia, The Perennial Heresy.* New York: University Press of America. 1990.

Nichols, Stephen J., ed. *Jonathan Edwards' Resolutions and Advice to Young Converts.* Phillipsburg, NJ: P&R, 2001.

Noll, Mark. *The Scandal of the Evangelical Mind.* Grand Rapid, MI: Eerdmans, 1994.

Pontynen, Arthur. *For the Love of Beauty: Art History and the Moral Foundations of Aesthetic Judgment.* Piscataway, NJ: Transaction, 2006.

Pontynen, Arthur, and Rod Miller. *Western Culture at the American Crossroads: Conflicts over the Nature of Science and Reason.* Wilmington, DE: ISI, 2011.

Ramsden, Michael. "Calling the Humanist Bluff." October 15, 2015. Sovereignty Education and Defense Ministry. https://sedm.org/michael-ramsden-calling-the-humanist-bluff/.

———. "Q&A." Apirl 14, 2016. Salt & Light International Leaders Conferenc, Duluth, GA. https://www.youtube.com/watch?v=dIKNdkrhnJ4&t=1687s.

Rollins, Peter. "The Idolatry of God: Christ and the End of Religion." Lecture, University of Central Arkansas, January 31, 2012.

Root, Jerry. *C.S. Lewis and a Problem of Evil: An Investigation of a Pervasive Theme.* Eugene, OR: Pickwick, 2009.

Senz, Nicholas. "Buying Virtue." *The Catholic Thing* (blog), January 11, 2018. https://www.thecatholicthing.org/2018/01/11/buying-virtue/.

Siedell, Daniel A. *God in the Gallery: A Christian Embrace of Modern Art.* Grand Rapids, MI: Baker, 2008.

Spurgeon, Charles H. *Faith's Checkbook.* Issaquah, WA: Made For Success, 2014.

Warner, Nancy le Plastrier. *Hugh Compton Warner: The Story of a Vocation.* London: SPCK, 1958.

Warren, Richard. *Purpose Driven Church.* Grand Rapids, MI: Zondervan, 1995.

Weaver, Richard. *Ideas have Consequences.* Chicago: University of Chicago Press, 1948.

Willard, Dallas. *The Divine Conspiracy: Rediscovering Our Hidden Life in God.* London: HarperCollins, 1998.

Willey, Basil. *Christianity, Past and Present.* Cambridge: Cambridge University Press, 1952.

"Willow Creek Repents? Why the most influential church in America now says 'We made a mistake.'" *Christianity Today: Pastors,* October 18, 2007. Accessed August 19, 2019. https://www.christianitytoday.com/pastors/2007/october-online-only/willow-creek-repents.html.

Wilson, Jared C. *The Prodigal Church: A Gentle Manifesto against the Status Quo.* Wheaton, IL: Crossway, 2015.

Wilson, William G. *Alcoholics Anonymous: The Story of How More Than One Hundred Men Have Recovered from Alcoholism.* New York: Works, 1939.